Time Management

Unlock Unconventional Habits for Real Productivity, Focus, and Self-Discipline and Discover How to Beat Procrastination Once and For All

© Copyright 2019

All Rights Reserved. No part of this book may be reproduced in any form without permission in writing from the author. Reviewers may quote brief passages in reviews.

Disclaimer: No part of this publication may be reproduced or transmitted in any form or by any means, mechanical or electronic, including photocopying or recording, or by any information storage and retrieval system, or transmitted by email without permission in writing from the publisher.

While all attempts have been made to verify the information provided in this publication, neither the author nor the publisher assumes any responsibility for errors, omissions or contrary interpretations of the subject matter herein.

This book is for entertainment purposes only. The views expressed are those of the author alone, and should not be taken as expert instruction or commands. The reader is responsible for his or her own actions.

Adherence to all applicable laws and regulations, including international, federal, state and local laws governing professional licensing, business practices, advertising and all other aspects of doing business in the US, Canada, UK or any other jurisdiction is the sole responsibility of the purchaser or reader.

Neither the author nor the publisher assumes any responsibility or liability whatsoever on the behalf of the purchaser or reader of these materials. Any perceived slight of any individual or organization is purely unintentional.

Contents

INTRODUCTION 1
THE EVIL BEAST: PROCRASTINATION 3
PRIORITIZING TASKS 14
CUT OUT THE CRAP 20
SET UP YOUR ENVIRONMENT RIGHT 28
PLAN, PREPARE, EXECUTE 38
GET YOUR LIFESTYLE RIGHT 58
TRACK YOUR TIME 75
STREAMLINE COMMUNICATION 85
CONCLUSION 90

Introduction

I would like to thank you for choosing Time Management: Unlock Unconventional Habits for Real Productivity, Focus, and Self-Discipline and Discover How to Beat Procrastination Once and For All. The goal of this book is to help you beat the demon of procrastination so that you can get things done when needed instead of waiting until the last moment and rushing through them.

The first stop we will make on our journey is to look at what procrastination is. While, in theory, procrastination may seem simple to define, it is a little more complex. It is not caused by laziness, as some people believe.

After we cover procrastination, the rest of the book will focus on techniques that will help you to overcome procrastination. First, you will learn how to prioritize your tasks. Sometimes the biggest task is not the most important, so it is important to learn how to figure out what is. Then we will look at the importance of cutting back on the tasks you need to accomplish. For a long time, people have been fed the lie that the only way to be successful is to get a lot of stuff done. That is simply not true, and sometimes the best thing you can do is decide not to do something.

Next, we will go over setting up your environment so that it works for productivity. Sometimes the only thing standing in our way is a cluttered desk, so making sure you have a clean, productive environment is all it takes. Then we will go over creating a plan for what you are going to do, when, and how.

Next, we will look at your lifestyle. Believe it or not, your health, sleep, diet, and nutrition all play a huge role in your productivity. We will look at the best sleeping and eating habits that will help to improve your productivity. Then we will look at the importance of tracking how you use your time. Many apps are available to tell you exactly how you have been using your time so you can ensure you are using it wisely.

Lastly, we will go over streamlining communication. A big problem within the business is the world is communication, and the main cause of miscommunication is having huge work teams. We will look at how to fix this problem.

The Evil Beast: Procrastination

While many people like to blame procrastination on the internet, procrastination has been happening for a long time now. People have struggled with the need to hesitate to date all the way to ancient civilizations. At around 800 BCE, Hesiod, a Greek poet, cautioned us never to "put your work off till tomorrow and the day after." Cicero, a Roman consul, referred to procrastination as "hateful" when it came to affairs. Those are just a couple of examples in recorded history. Who knows, maybe the dinosaurs noticed the meteorite falling to Earth but decided to return to their game of Rock Crush.

Procrastination is "the practice of carrying out less urgent tasks in preference to more urgent ones or doing more pleasurable things in place of less pleasurable ones and, thus, putting off impending tasks to a later time." For something to be considered procrastination, it must be damaging, delaying, and needless.

What has become very clear since Cicero's days is that procrastination is more harmful than hateful. Many studies have discovered that those who procrastinate will often have a lot more stress and a lower sense of well-being. Procrastination may cause negative results such as not having enough retirement savings or missing important doctor's appointments. H&R Block surveys have discovered that many people end up paying more for their taxes than they should because they waited until the last minute to complete them.

Over the last twenty years, there has been an increased interest in procrastination. Psychologists have now realized that there is a lot more to procrastination than just waiting to do something. True procrastination is some form of failure of self-regulation. Experts define procrastination as voluntarily delaying an important task that we want to accomplish, even though we know we will suffer due to the procrastination. Not having a complete grasp of time could increase this issue, but not being able to handle emotions is often the base of the problem.

Causes

Within clinical psychology, there seems to be a connection between a self-defeating mentality, low self-worth, and anxiety for procrastinators. However, most studies performed with people who do not need psychological services show a minimal connection between these problems and procrastination. Instead, procrastination has a very strong connection to a lack of self-confidence or just simply hating the task.

One of the strongest connections to procrastination is impulsiveness. These types of characteristics tend to be used to measure a person's conscientiousness traits, whereas irrational beliefs and anxiety are aspects of neuroticism. Being a perfectionist has no direct ties to procrastination. The consensus is that the main we procrastinate due to a breakdown in self-control. You realize you should be working on a certain task but cannot motivate yourself to do it. Professionals claim this is caused by a gap between intention and action.

A professor of psychology at DePaul University, Joseph Ferrari, said, "What I've found is that while everybody may procrastinate, not everyone is a procrastinator." He has become a pioneer in modern procrastination research and discovered that around 20 percent of people are considered chronic procrastinators. He explained that procrastination has very little to do with time-management. Telling a chronic procrastinator that they should just do it is like telling a clinically depressed person to get over it.

One of the main misconceptions concerning procrastination is that it is an unexplainable habit or that it might be helpful. People who sympathize with procrastination say it does not matter when something is finished as long as it gets done. Some people believe they work better under pressure. John Perry, a Stanford philosopher and author of *The Art of Procrastination*, explained that people could learn how to waste time in their favor by changing up what needs to be done so that something is always being accomplished. Psychologists have a big issue with this point of view. They argue that it combines helpful actions like pondering or prioritizing with the negative side effects of procrastination. If progressing through a task can be done in many ways, then procrastination is the complete and total absence of any progress.

Ferrari explained that if a person has a dozen things to accomplish, they might realize that the last three things need to wait. But a procrastinator may do a couple of them, rewrite the list, change the order, and then make another copy of their list. That is what procrastination looks like.

In 1997, a study published in *Psychological Science* was the first to evaluate the negative side effects of procrastination. Psychologists Roy Baumeister, William James, and Dianne Tice, then working at Case Western Reserve University, used a scale to rate the procrastination of college students. They tracked how the students performed in school, their stress levels, and their general health during the rest of the semester. Initially, it seemed procrastination had benefits because the procrastinating students had lower stress levels than those who did not procrastinate. They presumed this was because they did more pleasurable things when procrastinating. By the end of the study, however, the negative effects of procrastination were a lot bigger than the benefits. Procrastinators received lower grades than those who finished tasks on time, and they had higher levels of illnesses and stress. Procrastinators not only turned in their work late, but the quality also suffered as well as their well-being.

A few years later, Ferrari and Tice worked together on a study that explained procrastination's side effects. They assembled some college volunteers and told them they would be solving some math problems at the end of their session. Some participants were told the math test was very important and would score their cognitive ability, and the other participants were told that it was just a meaningless test. Before the tasks started, the students were given a little time to either study for the test or just play some games. It turned out that the chronic procrastinators only delayed studying for the test when they were told it was important. When they were told it was just for fun, they behaved just like non-procrastinators. Tice and Ferrari described their conclusions in the *Journal of Research in Personality* in 2000, stating that procrastination was self-demeaning. People who procrastinate simply try to undermine themselves and their efforts.

Intention and Action Gap

There is not just one type of procrastinator. Several general impressions have come out through years of research. The chronic procrastinator has a perpetual problem finishing things, while circumstantial procrastinators set back things based on the actual task. The worst combination of this happens when a person who has low self-discipline and high impulsivity meets an unpleasant task. Most delayers portray the actions of self-defeat because of some type of negative state, like perfectionism or fear of failure. But it can come from a positive side as well, like the joy of temptation. This is the reason many researchers refer to procrastination as the "quintessential" self-control breakdown.

People who have very high levels of impulsivity and lack discipline and self-control will likely notice that they procrastinate more than people who have developed their self-control. Normally, people have some form of ego control when they delay responsibility. They will then make excuses for their delay. These justifications serve a very important purpose. They give the person the chance to continue procrastinating by downplaying the consequences that their actions are causing and gives them the chance to feel good about who they are.

Social scientists, though, have debated if this gap could be described as not being able to manage their time or not having good control over their emotions and mood. Many people follow the explanation of procrastination described in *Psychological Bulletin* in 2007 by Piers Steel, a University of Calgary professor. His idea is that the procrastinator looks at the level of "fun" activities have. Those that are more pleasurable have more value, while tough tasks become more valuable the closer their deadline gets.

On the other hand, psychologists like Pychyl and Ferrari see the flaws in this temporal view. For example, if the delay were a rational thought as this view suggests, then this behavior would not need to be called procrastination. It would be more accurate to call it time management. Besides that, several studies have found that people who procrastinate also feel guilt, anxiety, or shame in their choice of delaying action. This emotional component tells us there is more to the story than simple time management. Pychyl found how emotions and mood played into procrastination when he first started working on this during the '90s, and then solidified his idea when he published his study in the *Journal of Social Behavior and Personality* in 2000. For his study, he had forty-five undergraduates keep a pager on them, and they tailed them during the five days leading up to a very important test. The participants were beeped eight times a day, and each time, they reported their level of procrastination and emotional state. As their prep for the test became harder and more stressful, the students would put them off for things that were more pleasing. When they did this, they also expressed a higher level of guilt, which was a hint that they still had some feelings of dread for the important work they had pushed to the side. Pychyl concluded that procrastinators recognized the harm in their actions, but they could not avoid the emotional need for distraction.

Another study, published *in the Journal of Personality and Social Psychology* in 2001, reinforced the role that mood played. Tice and his team found that students would not procrastinate before a big assessment if they were told that their mood would stay fixed. But when they thought that their mood might change, they put off studying until the last minute. His findings showed that a person's self-control would only break down when a person thought their emotions could be improved.

In general, people learn from their mistakes, and they will take a different approach to problems. When it comes to chronic procrastinators, this way of looking at things does not work correctly. This problem does not allow them to realize they need to start working on things earlier. Figuring out the explanation for this behavior lies within the emotional aspect of procrastination. Ironically, a need to get rid of stress during the moment causes a procrastinator to try to figure out how to fix this problem.

A few years ago, Fuschia Sirois recruited eighty students to participate in a study and evaluated them for procrastination. The partakers read about trying events caused by unnecessary delay. One of the scenarios had a person coming back from a holiday to find a suspicious-looking mole, but they did not go to the doctor right away, which created a worrisome situation.

Afterward, Sirois asked the participants for their thoughts on the scenario. She discovered the procrastinators in the group said things like, "At least they went to the doctor before it got worse." This is called a downward counterfactual and tells you that a person wants to improve their mood within a short-term period. Also, these same people very rarely said things like, "If only they had gone sooner." This is what is called an upward counterfactual and shows the real tension within a moment to try to learn something. Basically, procrastinators would focus on the best way to feel better because of memories that make them feel worse.

Pychyl and Sirois recently tried to bring together the emotional and temporal aspects of procrastination. They shared a two-part theory about procrastination in an issue of *Social and Personality Psychology Compass* that connects the short-term improvements in mood with time-related, long-term problems. The belief is that those who procrastinate try to comfort themselves in the present while also using false beliefs that they will be emotionally prepared in the future.

Common Justification

One key finding about procrastination is that procrastinators make justifications for their actions or, rather, the lack thereof. The individual coping responses to procrastination tend to be avoidance or emotional-oriented instead of problem-solving or task-oriented. Emotional coping is supposed to help reduce the stress that is connected to procrastination. This form of justification provides a person with pleasure and gives them the chance to draw attention away from the consequences.

The following are common ways that people excuse delaying what they should be working on.

- Valorization, or promoting better gains: A person points out the things they already achieved while they should be working on something else that is likely of great importance.

- Avoidance: A person avoids the situation or location where the task is taking place. This is not a verbal justification but a physical one. They physically make sure they are not there so they can say they could not work on it. They may avoid going in for meetings or choose to watch TV instead of cleaning their bedroom.

- Laziness: This does not mean the person is lazy, because they are not. The procrastinator is excusing their actions by saying they are lazy.

- Distraction: They take part in other actions or behaviors to prevent themselves from being aware of the task they should be working on.

- Denial: They pretend they are not really procrastinating because what they are doing is "more important" than what they are avoiding.

- Trivialization: They try to convince themselves that the actual task is not all that important.

- Reframing: They pretend that getting started early on a project is a bad thing and ditch their work until the last moment, believing it will give them exceptional outcomes.

- Comparisons: They compare their situation to one that is even worse.

- External Blaming: They blame the cause of their procrastination on external forces beyond their control.

- Humor: They make a joke about their lack of achievement and procrastination to avoid the effort that would be required to finish the work.

Procrastination and Neuropsychology

Over the years, procrastination studies have moved past personality, cognition, and emotion into the world of neuropsychology. It is well known that many frontal systems of the brain are involved in several processes that all have to do with self-regulation, which includes self-control, problem-solving, and planning. These are all considered to be executive functioning. Oddly, though, nobody had taken the time to examine a connection between these brain sections and procrastination.

Laura Rabin, from Brooklyn College, said, "Given the role of executive functioning in the initiation and completion of complex behaviors, it was surprising to me that previous research had not systematically examined the relationship between aspects of executive functioning and academic procrastination."

To fix this problem, Rabin and her colleagues brought together 212 understudies and studied them for procrastination traits. They then assessed them on the nine executive functioning subscales: general orderliness, working memory, emotional control, task monitoring, task initiation, activity shifting, organization and planning, self-monitoring, and impulsivity. The researchers involved thought they would find a link between certain subscales and procrastination. As it turned out, the procrastinators had a significant association with all them.

Rabin explained the limitation of the study. First, their findings were correlative, which means it is not clear if the executive functioning elements were the actual cause of the procrastination. They also used many self-reports for their assessments. It might, at some point, need to have functional imaging to expand or confirm the delay in the brain's center in real-time. This could still show that procrastination may be an "expression of subtle executive dysfunction" in those who are completely neurologically healthy.

Effects

It is worth really looking at the effects of procrastination. The experiences people have after wasting their time and not reaching deadlines hurt them on personal and business levels. Procrastination will likely create more stress, a loss of personal productivity, a feeling of crisis and guilt, as well as social and business disapproval for not meeting your responsibilities. All these feelings come together and cause even more procrastination.

For some people, the stress and anxiety that procrastination creates will motivate them to take action. However, people normally follow this by trying to justify their reasons for delaying their actions, which helps reinforce this behavior. It is common for people to procrastinate to a small degree, but to completely give up procrastinating, they will have to rise above the attempts to minimize or justify their actions as being acceptable.

Within some psychological circles, people believe that chronic procrastination signals an underlying disorder. Others see procrastination as a great way of identifying what is most important to a person because it is rare to procrastinate on something that you truly love.

However, a procrastinator needs to learn how to increase the value of their preferences, even if they do not enjoy them, so they will continue to be valuable in every aspect of their lives. The general view of procrastination is that task-aversion is caused by low ambition, willpower, and irresponsibility. While people who study procrastination know this is not true, this is still how the public views procrastinators.

Interventions

As our understanding of procrastination grows, researchers hope to see a greater effect with an intervention. With the work on executive functioning, there may be several remedies for unwanted delay. Procrastinators could break their large tasks into smaller pieces to manage them better. Counseling could help people notice that they are compromising their goals for quick pleasure. Coming up with a personal deadline works perfectly based on the research performed by Klaus Wertenbroch and Dan Ariely on "precommitment." In one issue of P*sychological Science* in 2002, they reported that procrastinators would set deadlines for themselves, and these deadlines did help them finish their tasks. These types of deadlines do not have as much of an effect as external ones, but they do help.

The emotional components of procrastination are harder to solve. Ways to counter temptations include getting rid of distractions, but the problem is that the effort to do this requires the self-regulation that procrastinators lack. Sirois believes that one of the best ways to get rid of the need to find a quick mood fix is to find a part of the task that is worthwhile or positive.

Ferrari would like to see a change in rewarding the early birds instead of punishing lateness. Among the several things that he proposed, he said there should be some incentive to file your taxes early by providing a break if a person filed before March 15. He also says we should quit enabling procrastination within personal relationships. While tough love might help with couples, one of the best solutions for the individual would be self-forgiveness.

In the end, procrastination has very little to do with laziness, but more to do with higher trait influences of avoiding what is seen as boring and impulsivity. Most people can spot procrastination when they are doing it. Humans can reflect on the things that they intend or need to do and then they can justify why they are not taking any action toward those things. Procrastination tends to occur most often when we fail to rule our hasty actions and absent the discipline we need to get ourselves back on track.

At its core, procrastination happens we let present emotional pleasures influence our motivations instead of focusing on the unpleasant emotional payoff of what needs to be done. It is important to grasp different approaches to changing our sentimental intensity toward certain goals to overcome procrastination and improve productivity.

Prioritizing Tasks

When it comes to productivity and ending procrastination, you must give priority to the task at hand. When you are not motivated, you will continue to put it off, no matter how important it is. There many helpful tips for prioritizing tasks. People will tell you to get the most important thing done first, and that is fine, but what is most important to one person may not be to you. That is what prioritizing your tasks is all about. We will talk later about "eating the frog" and the 80/20 rule, but first, let us look at a basic way of prioritizing.

Let us say you have a long to-do list, but you do not know what you should start with and you do not currently feel motivated to do any of it. Before you can ever prioritize your to-do list, you must organize it. There is no one way to organize these things, so make sure you choose something that makes sense to you.

Once you have organization under control, you can move on to prioritization. Not every single task has the same level of importance. The most important task is the one that will move you closer to your long-term goals. Prioritizing gives you the chance to find the most important task at any given moment so you can give it your full attention, time, and energy. This ensures that you will spend your time on the right things.

Prioritization gives you the chance to plan things. It makes sure that your deadlines are met and you minimize stress. The first thing you need to do is make a list of everything you need to complete. When you have large projects, find small tasks that will help to move the project forward. You should be able to finish the tasks within a few hours or a couple of days. Depending on how you decide to break things down, your list could include what you can do in one day or over several weeks.

Then go through and write down the due dates of these items. Divide your tasks between long-range, midrange, due within the next week, or next month. After you have done this, you will assign a priority to every task, from the most urgent things to the not so important. Designate their levels of importance with an A, B, C, and so on. After you have specified their levels of importance, rank each task within each level using a secondary designation, like B-1, B-2, B-3. Some people will continue to make levels, but it usually works better if you do what feels natural to you.

Now figuring out which items are the most important can be either simple or hard. For items whose importance you are not sure about, I have some questions that can help you sort them out. Then you can figure out which ABC level they belong in.

Why is the task important?

I know everything on the list needs to be done, but if you cannot come up with a good reason for them, you will need to be motivated enough to do it. If you want to finish something on that list, it must matter to you. You must find meaning in the things you need to do. So write down the reasons why the task is important. Is it going to help somebody? If so, who will it help? Will it have an impact on the world? Or will it make you more successful?

In what direction will this task take you?

This will give you direction as to where these tasks will take you. How the future looks will provide you with purpose. It provides you with aspirations, which can help to motivate you. And this can be a big goal too, several years into the future, if you want.

How you are going to get there?

This is how you are going to finish the task and reach your aspiration. This part is grounded in your current reality—what you can get done now to move you closer to your goals.

By this point, you should have a list of what you need to do and have organized within levels of importance. Now, if you have several reports to write out, journal articles to read, or accounts to pay, I would suggest grouping them into a single block and completing them as a group as opposed to spreading them out.

Begin and end your day with your to-do list. Check the things off that you have finished and then review what tasks remain. However, do not start reprioritizing your list. This can just turn into another excuse for procrastination. Once you set your priority levels, do not change them unless something drastic happens and certain items rise significantly in importance.

There may be a time when you are faced with conflicting priorities. As humans, we face multiple demands on our time each day. Oftentimes, the volume or rank of the requestor upsets our schedule, which can cause a loss of control. In situations like these, how do you figure out your priorities? The first thing you should do is ask questions. Everybody thinks their project is the most important, and they want it done immediately. With some strategic questions, along with some empathy, you can find a more accurate time frame and priority level for the task. When multiple people are involved within a single project, you need to figure out where your part of the puzzle fits in with the overall project. If you have to come up with data that another person analyzes, this is going to need a longer lead-time than just creating a simple document.

Taking charge of time and space will give you the chance to focus on the things that are important, minimize stress, and meet deadlines.

Eat That Frog

If you have never heard of this before, you are probably a little confused as to what frogs and priorities have to do with each other. The concept of eating a frog came from this Mark Twain quote: "If it's your job to eat a frog, it's best to do it first thing in the morning.

And if it's your job to eat two frogs, it's best to eat the biggest one first."

In a sense of priorities, your frog is the biggest and most important thing you need to do. It is the one thing that you will probably be the most likely to procrastinate on. If you have two frogs, eat the biggest first. This is simply another way of saying that if there are two equally important tasks, start with the hardest or the biggest. Discipline yourself to start working on it immediately and then persist until you have finished the task before you move onto something else.

One of the most helpful things in the world of reaching high levels of productivity and performance is to create the habit of taking care of your most important task first thing every day. You must come up with the habit of "eating your frog" before you start doing anything else and without getting hung up on thinking about it. This is a habit that many successful people have adopted and is an essential leadership quality.

Successful people start working on their biggest tasks and then make sure that they work steadily on that single task until it is complete. Not executing something is a major problem within business today. Many people confuse activity with accomplishment. People will continuously talk, go to a countless number of meetings, and come up with plans, but nobody has finished the job and gotten the results needed.

For example, if you have always wanted to write a book, it will not happen until you change your wants from a dream to a goal. And even when you do, you still need to take action.

Your dreams won't do any good until you start taking action on them, come up with goals, and learn how to write a good book. This is also true with any other idea that comes to mind, so make sure that you act quickly on your intuition and start with whatever task will help you be the most productive.

The 80/20 Rule

The last thing we are going to look at for prioritizing your tasks is the 80/20 rule. Vilfredo Federico Damaso Pareto, who was born in 1848 in Italy, thought up this concept. He went on to become an economist and philosopher. Legend has it that he was caring for his pea plants and found that 20 percent of the plants generated 80 percent of the healthy pea pods. This caused him to start thinking about uneven distribution. He began to think about wealth and found that 80 percent of Italy's land was owned by only 20 percent of the actual population. He investigated several industries and discovered that 80 percent of production came only from 20 percent of the companies. The following generalization grew from this: 80 percent of your results will originate from 20 percent of the action.

The "universal truth" about the differences between inputs and outputs is what turned into the Pareto principle, or the 80/2o rule. While everything does not always come out to be perfect 80/20 ratio, you can still see this imbalance in various business models.

- 80% of all sales are generated by 20% of the sales reps.
- 80% of all profits come from 20% of customers.
- 80% of software crashes are caused by 20% of software bugs.
- 80% of healthcare spending comes from 20% of patient accounts.

You can probably look at different aspects of your life and see the 80/20 rule at work. Think about the clothes you own and how often you only pick a certain 20 percent of the outfits to wear. Look at the rooms in your house. You like to spend 80 percent of your time in only 20 percent of the rooms. The same is likely true about the roads in your town and the apps on your phone.

If you sat down and talked with hundreds of successful people, Olympic athletes, and straight-A students and asked them how they handled all their tasks, they would say it is impossible to handle all of them. They make use of this 80/20 rule to help them figure out what is important. The rest gets delegated or forgotten about.

So how can you use this to improve your time usage?

If you are an executive, you are probably constantly faced with the challenge of limited resources. You do not just need to maximize your time, but your entire team's. Instead of trying to do things that are impossible, the 80/20 rule can help you to understand what projects are important. What goals are the most important for your business, and which tasks will help to push you closer to your goals? Get rid of the rest or have somebody else do them.

If you are a freelancer, it is a good idea to identify your best clients. You do not need to place all your eggs in a single basket. If you have too many clients, you can easily get burned out. Focus on the people who will make you the money and improve those long-term relationships.

If you are an entrepreneur, there is always a temptation to do something exciting and new. There is nothing wrong with this, but it should all come down to your goals. Do you want to grow your current business? Using the 80/20 rule will help you stay focused so you do not waste your time chasing down endless opportunities.

No matter what situation you are in, it is important to remember that each day has a certain number of hours in it, and only so many days in a week. The Pareto principle can help you see this as a good thing. If you don't try this, you may find that you are always stuck in a never-ending to-do list.

So what is the 20 percent of your work that drives 80 percent of your outcomes?

Cut Out the Crap

This chapter piggybacks onto the last, especially with the 80/20 rule. We are going to talk about how the biggest help in time management is to do less, not more. There is an endless supply of information about how to be more productive. Books, apps, seminars, and more promise to give you the key to productivity; however, these things give you a reason to procrastinate. They will force you to try to get everything done and switch between tasks, but you never really get anything done.
The key to getting things done is to just do them. It is as simple as that. But so many "tools" have you are sitting around for hours or days on end trying to optimize the best way to do things without ever getting started. Instead, you need to clear things out of your life and clear things off your plate to get things done. Some things are just not important enough to waste your time and energy on.
What if I said you could only work for ninety minutes every single day, but you had to be just as productive as you are right now? While this might sound like some science fiction scenario, in practice, it is easy to do.
In America, the typical office worker only finished about ninety minutes of actual work each day. The rest of the time they are doing things like reading the paper, socializing with others, taking a break,

reorganizing things, and answering unimportant emails. What is worse is when you really look at the tasks that make up those ninety minutes; most of it consists of redoing work to make it "right" for the company.

The same is still true for people who are not office workers and are working on personal projects. In general, the longer we think we are going to work on a certain task, the more that time gets filled with things that are not helpful like meetings or research.

If a person decides to work on their blog for eight hours, they will start redesigning it, changing old posts for readability, researching things, and so on. These things may be helpful, but they are not necessary. Now, if the same person were told to work on their blog for three hours, they would get an article written during the first two and spend the rest of the time on marketing.

The main reason this happens is that we are all stuck in a mindset that worked one-hundred years ago but does not work for most of our modern jobs. In a factory setting, the number of things that are produced is directly related to the number of hours a person works. Restaurants and stores are in similar situations. But this principle does not apply to social or creative jobs. In those cases, when it comes to an hour of productivity and an hour of distraction, there is a huge difference.

While ninety-minute workdays are not ideal, it also does not make sense to spend more time working when it is only going to cause us to be less productive. No matter how many hours you work, the message is that you need to be relentless in evaluating your tasks and refuse to work on anything without a clear purpose. It does not matter if you assign yourself the task, or your boss does. Ditch those meetings unless you have found that they are effective. If you have to, communicate your reasons for doing this, and then ask people to brief you on them after if anything was of importance.

The biggest unproductive trait people have is that they second-guess themselves. A person can spend a large amount of time questioning decisions they have already made. You have made the decision, so let it go. Just do whatever you planned. Do not allow yourself to get bogged down in analyzing all your decisions.

Everybody has the same twenty-four hours in a day to get things done. All we have to work with is our energy. Now, if you take that energy and expend it on a bunch of different projects, each of those projects will get a little of your energy. If you eliminated all but one of those projects, then all those little pieces of energy get grouped together, and all that energy goes to that single project. So that one project is progressing exponentially more than those millions of projects getting a little of your energy. Which sounds better to you?

If you spend all your energy on a bunch of different things, you will get nowhere fast. But if you choose to pare down your tasks every day, you will be able to make exponential progress toward your ultimate business or life goal.

For example, Olympic swimmer Michael Phelps' to-do list is to wake up and get in the pool. His goal was to be the world's best swimmer, and he understood that the only way to accomplish that was by practicing his swimming. Instead of wasting his time on social media and other things, he got into the pool and swam.

Now, you do not have to just have one goal in life, but you do need to have just one thing to focus on. You can move on to another when the first one is done. We are going to look at some things you can do to pare down your tasks and get you moving toward your goals.

Personal Life

Now, before you get mad, let me explain myself. I am not talking about giving up your personal life. You can still have your social media, parties, vacations, or whatever you like to do for fun. Everybody needs those things; otherwise, you are going to simply burn out. I am talking about those things that tend to interrupt our "business" life or our journey toward our dreams.

So often, people will stop what they are doing because they remember an errand they need to run. Things like cooking, cleaning, laundry, gardening, grocery shopping, and the like can take away our valuable time. These things must be done, but there are ways to schedule them so you can stay focused on your tasks, projects, and dreams and help them to progress.

Let us look at how you can handle grocery shopping and cooking. If you are already making $10,000 or more each month, then you could simply hire somebody to take care of these things for you, and then you would just have to take the time to eat. But a more realistic approach for most people is to pick one day a week—Sundays normally work best—to go grocery shopping and then prep all your meals for the week. That way, all you have to do is grab your meals out of the fridge or freezer, heat it up, and eat it. This reduces your wasted time so that you can focus on what is most important. You can do the same for all your other personal tasks. Figure out a day of the week where you can take care of those things, and only do it on those days.

There are a lot of stress-inducing bits of information online that share "tips" on how to get rid of these personal tasks. People tell you to hire others to take care of things for you so that all you have to think about is work. While that probably will help, it is not feasible for everybody. Not everybody has an extra $1,000 or more each month lying around to have a personal chef, gardener, maid, and so on. That is why it is important to learn how to schedule these things, and we will talk about schedules later so that they do not interfere with your work.

These things do not need to cause you more stress. Finding ways to get them done and not use them as a reason to procrastinate is the most important thing. You will learn exactly what that means for you as this book continues.

Be Proactive

People often make everybody's priorities their own, and 99 percent of the time, the emails you receive are not your priority. It is likely somebody else's job, yet people often stop their own work to work on somebody else's because they think they should. This is true in your business and personal life.

This is why you must be proactive with your priorities. You must plan the things you know you need to focus on to avoid taking on everybody else's tasks. Taking Sunday evening to come up with your priorities for the next week will change your life immensely. This means you will be starting your life with perfect clarity on what is most important for you and increase your odds of completing tasks. You will not allow yourself to be pulled in a million different directions.

What Brings You Your Goals?

Whether you have personal goals, like buying a new house, losing weight, or running a marathon, or you have professional goals, like making a career change, starting a blog, or getting a promotion, a task is only important if it moves you closer to that goal. During your work hours, whatever that means to you, focus only on the things that will move you closer to your business goals, nothing else. If you have many things on your to-do list, sort them from most to least important.

If you would like to increase your business's profits, stop trying thousands of different ideas. Pick a couple that will have the biggest impact and work on executing them well. Only change your strategies if you know for certain that one strategy is not working.

What Will Make Things Disappear?

Focus on tasks that will make other tasks easier, faster, or obsolete. Now, this can be a bit difficult to execute. To do this, look at the things you think you need to do and look for long, inefficient, tedious tasks. Come up with a way to get eliminate them and make them easier to accomplish.

Avoid These No-No's

Certain items people put on their to-do lists should not be there and will waste their time more than it will help. There are three main items that I would like you to eliminate from your to-do list from now on.

1. Email Catch-Up

Most of us will add items to our literal or mental to-do lists that we never planned to do in advance. This could be because we did not see it coming, or we do not think it will take long to do. Not surprising, catching up on those emails is one of the worst to fall into this category.

Some productivity experts say that blocking out a certain time period for going through emails is the best thing you can do. You do nothing else during this time but answer emails. But those same experts also say you need time away from your email to work on other things. This method works for some, but for others, it can create an issue that they use their to-do list to fix. When you are taking time away from your email, the inbox will continue to expand in the background, and those messages must be read, answered, or deleted. A person may add "catch up on emails" to their tasks when it may not be a good idea.

Instead, find a tool that can decrease how many emails you are getting. The good news is, you already have that tool. It is called your voice. If you look at the messages in your inbox right now, you will probably notice that around 20 percent of your current threads run to five or more people. After you have already established a full-on conversation with a person through email, you are using up a lot of your time doing something that could be done faster if you just talked to the person in person.

Instead of spending your time catching up on all those emails, pick up the phone or walk to somebody's office. Your short chat with them will be much more productive than the drawn-out conversation you will have through a series of emails. People also tend to like you more after you have an in-person conversation with them.

2. Multitasking

There is such a constant influx of work that it can be very hard to focus for long on a single task. So you start to work on that major report, and then twenty minutes later, you are going between that report and your emails, and then you are checking your texts, and then you may add a couple of other tasks on top of those. You might even just drag your laptop into your meeting so you can continue to work on whatever you started. You have heard that multitasking is inefficient and drains you cognitively, yet you continue to do it.

It would be different if you were achieving your important goals, but your to-do list shows that you really are not. That means you need to look at that list and mark off anything that you were planning on doing in tandem with other things. Those things can wait. Forcing yourself to focus on just the thing that you can "monotask" is one of the best ways to prioritize.

You should also put that smartphone away. Put it in your bag or lock it in your desk drawer. Remove any distractions you can to give yourself a fighting chance to meet your goals.

3. That Item that Just Came Up

Despite your best efforts, there will still be tasks that come up out of nowhere and will throw plans out of whack for the day. You must learn to say "no" to these requests. Everybody wants to help people from time to time, especially early on in your career. You might take extra steps to make a great impression on the person who will decide if you will get a promotion or raise.

If you look over your to-do list and find that you keep writing down new things to do, especially at the last minute, you are in big trouble. The problem is that you cannot impress a person if you do not do what is expected of you. You must be willing to say "no," but you also must understand how to say it. When a higher-up asks you to do something that will use up the time you need to accomplish your original work, discuss it with them.

There is no need to be apologetic or defensive with them. Just inform them of your current priorities and ask where their request fits in. Usually, once you have explained your position, they will ask somebody else or take something else off your plate so you can help them. These tradeoffs and collaborations can provide you with the breathing room you need.

Five Decisions

The last way to reduce your tasks is to follow one of these five basic decision-making tactics.

1. DO what they want you to do.

2. DELEGATE the task to somebody else who is either better qualified or has the time to do it.

3. DEFER the item or schedule it to be done later.

4. FILE it away to reference later.

5. DELETE it completely and just forget that it ever existed.

It is as simple as that, though I am fully aware that it is easier said than done. Once you have gotten used to doing things a certain way for years, it is hard to make this drastic change. But you can do it. With intentional action, you can change the way you handle your time.

The main thing I want you to remember is that you do not have to do everything. Doing more does not mean you are more successful. Doing more means you are making slow progress toward your goals and you stay burned out. Cut out anything that won't immediately help you in your goals. Plan your week so your personal work does not get in the way of your business work. By planning, which we will cover later, you can have a successful life with less stress. That is what time management can do for you.

Set Up Your Environment Right

Whether you work at home or in an office, your environment is very important. If you do work at home, it can be a bit harder. You do not have to worry about the commute and you can wear whatever you want to, but it requires way more dedication and self-motivation. But I am not here to advocate for working from home. I want to talk about your environment.

People think that big things interrupt productivity, but really, it is the small things that happen during the day. The biggest player in this is your environment.

Small things, like looking for a charger, may only take a couple of seconds or a minute to do, but it takes you thirty minutes or more to get back into a working mindset. You want the space you are working in to be effective and inspiring.

If the space in which you work does not spark inspiration and motivation, it will be very hard to get any work done.

Productive Office Space

Businesses want their employees to be more productive, but when you are in an office setting, what does that look like? Being productive does not mean that you get from A to B in a fast amount of time. Instead, it is about getting there in the most efficient way possible while keeping your sanity. A person's personal workspace tends to be an overlooked factor in productivity. Whether you are scrounging through the drawers looking for some document, or you have too many knick-knacks on your desk, having an efficient desk setup is important for success.

1. Create a chance for movement.

One of the best ways to stay focused is to notice when you have hit a productivity wall. When you do, taking a short walk can help you find a new perspective. Research also backs this up. Several studies have found that breaking up your workday with mental rest periods can help improve productivity. Taking quick walks during the day can help lower your stress levels and boost your health.

Having a desk that can go from sitting to standing can help, and many offices allow these. You can do other things that will allow you to move as well. Having the phone and copy machine in another room or some distance away and a central place to get water, coffee, and other refreshments will give you a reason to walk around.

2. Add a plant to your desk.

Sometimes making a simple change can have a huge effect on your productivity, such as keeping a small plant in your office or at your desk. This helps make your space feel alive. houseplants are effective methods of aiding in productivity. In 2014, a research team in the UK discovered that having a plant in the office would boost productivity by 15 percent, as well as improve satisfaction in the workplace and work engagement.

3. Give your gadgets a place to live.

Tablets, smartphones, and other such gadgets can aid in organization and efficiency. But they are also a great way to waste time. Studies have discovered that smartphones have a negative effect on productivity. In one survey, it was discovered that workers spent five hours each week doing things on their phones that did not have to do with work.

The best way to avoid this distraction is to find a place to leave your gadgets while you are working. This could be a drawer you clear out to store your gadgets. If you cannot see them, then you will not be tempted to use them.

4. Clean your space daily.

Having a tidy workspace can aid in productivity. Throw out items that are not needed and maintain your organization system so that you have no extra distractions. Having a messy workspace will cause more problems than new ideas. Research has found that many employees spend about thirty-eight hours looking for misplaced or lost items every single year. That is almost an entire workweek.

Besides organizing and cleaning your space each day, take some time at the end of the day to organize your to-do list so you will know what to do the next day.

5. Personalize your area in moderation.

Giving your office space a personal touch can help improve your emotional connection to your work, but make sure you do not add too much because you do not want to be cluttered. Find a balance between meaningful and useful items. A desktop calendar might be helpful. You can also add a picture of somebody or something that inspires you.

6. Keep yourself comfortable.

In the perfect world, you would be able to control the temperature in your space for your optimum comfort level. Unfortunately, if you work in an office building, this is not possible, but there are some things you can do. First, see if you can request the thermostat be set to a warmer temp. One study from Cornell University found that temperatures under 68 Fahrenheit can cause more errors and reduce productivity. Meanwhile, temperatures above 68 can aid in productivity. Keep a jacket or sweater in your office in case you cannot do anything about the temperature.

7. Choose the right music or none at all.

For many people, the best way to get into their work is to put on some noise-canceling headphones and blast some music. Many studies have proven how effective this approach is. It can be difficult to figure out just the right music; however, using Pandora or Spotify can make it easier because they have playlists specifically made for productivity.

If music does not help, then that is fine. In fact, some studies have argued that music can be distracting. If you find it hard to concentrate when there is music playing, then embrace the silence.

    8. Add some things that are yellow.

Most office buildings are full of dull grays and neutral colors. While this color scheme is not at all distracting, it does not help to stimulate people in any way. Within the color theory, red is considered the most stimulating. However, red also carries a lot of negative connotations, like anger. One of the best colors to improve your workspace and make it more stimulating is yellow. It gives you just as much productivity as red, but it does not come with the negative side effects.

Desk Space

We have touched a little on what is on your desk, but let's really look at how your desk should look to make sure that you stay productive and not distracted. Everything we will discuss applies both to those who work at home and those who work in an office building.

You will be staring at what's on your desk for 50 percent of your day, so you might as well make sure it is filled with things that motivate you and aid in productivity.

    1. Plants

I said it above, and I will say it again, having a plant makes your space feel more alive. You do not even have to have a real plant. You can use a fake plant as well.

    2. Candles

You might not be able to have lighted candles if you work in an office building, but you do not even have to light it. Candles, especially scented ones, help relax you and put you at peace. This can help you get your ideas flowing. The look of candles just makes your desk look fancy.

3. Inspirational quotes or prints

If you have a wall, hang these on your wall. While it may sound cheesy, having some inspirational quotes or creative prints around can help motivate you during the day and help you out of a slump.

4. Framed photos

Framed photos are probably one of the first things that people will add to their desks. You can fill the frame with family members, pets, or whatever inspires and motivates you to continue working.

5. Colorful pens

You never know when you'll need to write something down, so having pens within arm's length is a good idea. Pens in different colors are fun to have.

6. Weekly planners and post-its

Post-it is the perfect thing to have around to jot down quick ideas and notes. Weekly planners help keep you organized or will make your brain believe that you are organized. You can also make these colorful to liven up your workspace.

7. Noticeboards

Noticeboards are great because you can fill them with so many things. To-do lists, calendars, post-it's with important notes, photos, funny memes, and reminders can be added to them, and so much more. You can also get these in several colors as well.

8. Dress up your computer

You are staring at it for most of the day, so why not make it look nice? Get a laptop cover and decal. This is a great way to distinguish your computer from others', and it livens up your office space as well. The keyboard decal can help protect your computer from dirt and anything else that might hit your keys. Plus, it can make you feel like you have a brand-new computer.

9. Lamp

Having a desk lamp is helpful if you plan on working late into the night. Nobody wants to work late, but sometimes it happens, and sometimes that is simply when inspiration hits. Having a lamp is necessary when working in the dark winter months and during the evenings. Nobody is looking to get a headache from bad lighting.

10. Snacks

Stopping to get something to eat can interrupt people several times a day. Having your snacks already at your desk, like nuts or fruit, is a great idea. This way, you will not have to get up when you feel a little hungry. It is also a good idea to keep a water bottle or two near you.

11. Trashcan

There are two reasons for having a trashcan nearby. First, it will keep your desk from getting cluttered so you can keep it organized. Second, it will improve your productivity so you do not have to stop your work to walk to a trashcan someplace else.

12. Calendar

Calendars mean you are organized and being organized means productivity. Having a calendar right in front of you will help you see what you have planned for the month. This way you do not have to search through your phone or computer to find your schedule; it will simply be right there.

Home Office

While the rules for your environment discussed above are universal, you can follow some special rules for a home office setup. As I stated above, it takes a lot more motivation and focus to work from home, so it is very important that your environment work for you and not against you.

1. Add a calming scent to your room.

This cannot necessarily be done in a regular office, but you can do this in a home office. Using scented candles, incense, or essential oils like jasmine and lavender can help give you some natural mental boosts. Aromatherapy might just be what will help you to get back on track.

2. Find a location in your home that works best for you.

This could be a whole other room or a section of the room. Decide if you want your desk facing the wall or at a window. Figure what space will work best for you. Everybody is a bit different. Some people find working at their kitchen table works for them. Some people will work in their bedroom, and some people will use their living room coffee table. If you do have a separate room to set up a home office, you can create your own little work oasis to have a motivating and inspiring space that helps you stay on track. If you can only use a section of an existing room, fear not; you can still create an amazing office spot.

3. Place yourself close to a power outlet.

Today, we all have phones and laptops, and if you are working, you'll need a laptop. We rely on having a full battery in order to work. Make sure that your laptop and phone is always fully charged by ensuring that you set your desk up close to a power outlet. If you cannot do that, then invest in an extension cord so you never have to let a low battery slow you down.

4. Make sure you have a well-lit office space.

You do not want to stress your eyes by working in the dark. Make sure you have a well-lit home office, and it is even better if it is natural light. After having that morning cup of coffee, natural light will help wake you up each morning. In addition, it would not hurt to have a desk lamp because the sun will not always come perfectly through the window.

5. Add in some personal motivating touches.

One of the best benefits of working from home is that you can decorate your office and workspace however you would like. If you want to plaster your wall with pictures of your family on vacation, then do so. Will pictures of future vacation spots motivate you? Hang them up as well. Adding in some green plants can also help liven up space and provide you with fresh air. If plants make you sneeze, then pick something different. Maybe you like candles or you just want a simple blank room—whatever works for you, add it. The main thing is not to add things that will constantly catch your attention and distract you from what you should be working on.

6. Do not have any televisions in your office space.

Yes, TVs are a great thing for relaxation or great background noise when cleaning the house, but they are not the best friend of a productive work environment. Even working near your living room where you can hear the TV playing can easily distract you, especially if you know it is your favorite show. The TV is an easy thing to get sucked into. They are an easy way to unwind from a long day, but you should not let that happen when you are supposed to be working. However, if you can stop yourself after just thirty minutes to an hour, you can enjoy some TV during your lunch break—just another perk of working from home.

7. Make sure that you stay comfortable.

You will likely be sitting on your butt most of the day, so make sure your seat is comfortable. While we are working on this, you should increase productivity along with sitting comfortably. Bring your laptop up to eye level if you have to. Working from home can provide you with many added benefits to enhance your comfort level. You do not have to listen to people complain about the air conditioning or feel the cold winter's breeze whip through an open window because somebody was too hot.

You can also do some desk workouts and walk around a bit from time to time to avoid staying hunched over your screen the entire day. You might notice that some offices encourage using a standing desk to bring their computers up to eye level. You can either purchase a standing desk to try out or a new cushion for your chair—do what makes you feel at ease.

8. Get rid of as many distractions as you can.

You will know if your space is working for you by how much work you are able to get done. Try out a couple of different spaces in your house to see which one is working for you. While gazing out into your garden every day may seem romantic, it may cause you to spend more time staring out the window than doing any actual work. If you have outdoor animals, it may not be a good idea to sit where you can see them because you may be watching them play all day long.

Try to find a space where you will not be disturbed or bothered. Make sure you let your family know that they should not bother you when you are sitting in your office space and working. Whether this means that they are not allowed to come into your home office or bedroom until six, make sure they fully understand that you can't talk and play with them just because you work from home. If your phone easily distracts you, and you don't need it for work, leave it someplace else. You will be amazed at how much more work you can do when your office is phone free.

9. Dress like you are at the office.

While this might not be something that work-from-home people want to hear, wearing your pajamas may not be the best clothes for productivity. It is better to get dressed each morning before you start your day so you won't be surprised and panicked when you have to get dressed for a video call or go out. Plus, simply dressing the part can help you to feel more professional and tackle your work more efficiently.

Plan, Prepare, Execute

Every successful businessperson does one thing to stay focused and organized during their day: Each has a work routine.

If you have many tasks on your list, you might begin to feel overwhelmed and find it hard to get started. Having a routine will give you the structure you need to get a lot done in a short amount of time.

The point is not prioritizing your schedule but scheduling your priorities.

About 40 percent of your time at work is usually spent being unproductive. If you can create a routine and put some strategies into place, you can organize your day to drastically increase productivity.

Here are some tips to help you improve your schedule and productivity levels:

    1. Take a Break

Nobody can be productive 24/7. It is important to take breaks during the day to let your brain rest. By doing this, you can refresh yourself and be able to do more.

Alternating times of rest and activity are needed in order to survive and thrive. Mental endurance, interest, and capacity will wane and wax, so you need to plan accordingly.

2. Block Similar Tasks Together

Some people claim they are good at multitasking, but this is only a myth. Productivity will decrease by about 40 percent if you try to do more than two things at one time. But I do have a friend I have seen the talk on the phone while writing a blog post. This is very impressive since multitasking usually reduces the quality of work. Because our brains are switching between tasks, our attention also switches and we are not giving 100 percent to each task. Rather than trying to get several tasks done at one time, group similar tasks and do those in one-time chunks. This might mean making all phone calls in a specific hour or creating content at one time.

Time blocking means planning your day beforehand so you can dedicate certain hours of the day to accomplish certain tasks and determine when you need to have them done. When you know this, put these in your calendar and then work on them at the best time—midday. Time blocking your work will let you focus on whatever task you need to do to make you more productive during the day.

When you are organizing, make sure that you block out reactive and proactive blocks. Reactive blocks are the times you are allowing for any interruptions and requests like an emergency meeting and emails. Proactive blocks are the time you will be focusing on the important tasks you have to get done. This will be when you start to sketch out the prototype for your next project and draft documents or important projects.

You might want to place the most challenging task within the first couple of hours of the day and then look through your email in the afternoon. This prevents distractions, and you will know that you can deal with phone calls and emails later.

This method gives you the advantage of knowing exactly what you will be doing with your time and when you are going to be finishing chores. Simple to-do lists just provide you with a record of things you need to do. Time blocking gives you a list of things to do and provides you with a time to do them.

When you give yourself a rigid structure to work with and make yourself finish your tasks within this time frame, you are forcing yourself to be focused on everything you have to do. Planning your day beforehand on a calendar will help keep you focused on the things that matter most. No matter how you look at things, tasks take time.

3. Focus Sessions

If you keep jumping from one task to the next, you might feel busy, but you really are not getting a lot done. The best way to be productive is to take the largest task and schedule a time block to just focus on that one task.

Our minds are only able to deeply focus for a limited time, so you need to use that time for the most critical thinking. Performance and productivity are best during uninterrupted ninety-minute intervals, so try to schedule your time into ninety-minute blocks. Within each of these time blocks, do not work on any other task and stay away from distractions. Tell your coworkers you will be busy during this time and ask them nicely not to bother you. This way, you can stay focused without being interrupted.

Our bodies operate on ultradian rhythms. These cycles have peaks when we will be the most energized, and then a time when we tend to be more tired. By using ninety-minute sessions, you will take advantage of those peaks of energy that happen during the day. You will work for ninety minutes and rest for between twenty and thirty minutes. The rest period between work sessions is essential for improving.

Many people do not pay attention to their body's natural rhythms, and they use stimulants like coffee to help them power through their day. This usually causes a complete crash at about 2:30 p.m.

When you work in ninety-minute bursts, this will give you the chance to maximize your energy levels with the tasks that need to be completed and boost your productivity. Instead of working against your body, you will be working with it.

We have been trained by constantly working an eight-hour day to assume we have to work steadily from eight in the morning to five in the evening. You only get a break at lunch so you can exert your max output from the very beginning to the end of your day. While this helps managers remain on top of their workers, it will hurt productivity.

There are drawbacks to this system. You do not want your boss to find you lying on the floor of your cubicle taking a nap. They might not be happy, even if you told them that you were working with your natural rhythms and helping your memory. You could have deadlines that will cause you to have to work straight through.

When you are figuring out your schedule and not working against the clock, try working with your body's rhythm. You may find that your body does not work in ninety-minutes cycles, but you can monitor your natural energy for a couple of weeks to figure out what works best.

4. Eat the Frog

You are not going to literally eat a frog. This just refers to the thing you do not like to do but absolutely must do. You might not want to do it because it is either unpleasant or challenging. Most people will do whatever they can to keep from doing the things they dread. Being busy is used as a disguise to avoid important but uncomfortable tasks. If you "eat the frog" first thing in the morning rather than fretting about that task all day, the rest of the day will be easier and more productive. You will feel like a weight has been lifted from your shoulders. You will also feel accomplished, and you can now cross off that dreaded task.

5. Focus on Just Three Tasks Each Day

This is also called the "most important task method." It is all about focusing on what is most important. Instead of writing down a huge list of things to do and then trying to do it all, figure out the three most important tasks and concentrate on those things. You can do more than those three tasks, but you do not need to worry about anything else until those things have been finished.

On most days, only a couple of things need to be finished. You may have a bunch of voices trying to get your attention, but these are not important. The many notifications in your emails and on your phone can all wait. If you get those three most important tasks finished, everything else will become unnecessary.

When you have figured out the three most important tasks, schedule them in the first part of your day. You will be able to make some progress toward the most important tasks before you have to face all those distractions. This can be used along with time blocking if you would like, but save those first few hours for the important stuff. Meetings, phone calls, and emails can wait until you have finished. When you can focus on these tasks, your days will become more constructive. You will never have a day where you misuse your time on meaningless tasks.

If you are always working on small tasks and "putting out fires," you will not be able to work on your bigger goals. You can do this the night before or first thing each morning. Plan your schedule around these tasks and get rid of all distractions.

If you block out the hours between 9 and 11 to concentrate on your first task, turn off social media, email notifications, and your phone. If your office does not have a door, you can wear a pair of noise-canceling headphones. You could also work someplace quieter like a library or coffee shop.

It is easy to get caught up in the daily grind, but you must remember your largest goals. Staying away from distractions and not letting anybody interrupt you while you are working will keep you more productive. Most employees spend about two hours each day trying to recover from distractions.

    6. Plan Your Day

The average employee will spend about thirteen hours every week answering emails. If you check your email at the beginning of the day, it will take up all your time. when you could be doing something else. Many people spend a lot of time on things that are urgent but not enough time on things that are important. Before you open your email, take time to write down your tasks for the day and the things you want to accomplish. You can write this list at the end of the day to get ready for the next one. This allows you to get more things done and makes sure the work you are doing is enhances your business.

7. Morning Ritual

Every person's morning ritual will be different. Here is how some of the most successful people spend their mornings:

- Tony Robbins: He does not have a specific time to wake up. When he gets up, he jumps into a cryotherapy tank or the pool. He will then meditate and eat a breakfast high in protein.

- Richard Branson: He gets up at five each morning. He does cardio by running or playing tennis and has breakfast with the family. He will then read the news and check his email.

- Arianna Huffington: She does not use an alarm clock. She does not even check her phone until she has meditated for a few minutes.

- Oprah Winfrey: Once she gets up, she brushes her teeth, walks the dog, exercises, meditates, eats breakfast, and checks her schedule for the day.

- Mark Zuckerberg: He does not get up too early. Once he is up, he will either run or work out, eat breakfast, get dressed, and head to Facebook headquarters.

- Elon Musk: He spends thirty minutes reading important emails, he then gets a cup of coffee, takes a shower, and goes to the office.

8. Creating Your Routine

You can clearly see that no people have the exact same routine. It is about beginning your day the right way for you. If you want to create a morning routine, here are some ideas to get you started:

- Take time to do something you like to do: This might be working on a hobby, walking the dog, or eating breakfast. It will put things into perspective and put you in a good mood.

- Look over your calendar: When you do this, you know what to expect during the day. It ensures that you can address any conflicts before it is too late.

- Have goals for the day: If you can put your goals into words, you will have a 50 percent better chance to accomplish them. You will feel more in control over your life.

- Eat healthily, meditate, and exercise. You would think this is common sense to most people but staying in bed and eating doughnuts won't give you the energy you need to get through your day.

- Get up before everybody else: This will give you a chance to meditate, plan your day, write, read, or check your email without any distractions.

9. Don't Work in the Middle of the Day

The most productive people will plan their schedules around the time they are most productive. This means that if you are a night owl, then getting up early will be counterproductive. Because most people are productive during the morning, especially the few hours right after you wake up, it is not a bad idea to avoid working in the middle of the day.

Exercising is great for your energy levels and can make you more productive, but focus and energy will naturally ebb and flow during the day. If your focus is the best first thing, going to the gym would be a trade-off for your productive time. You could start going in the late afternoon or mid-morning. It might feel weird to start leaving the office in the middle of the day, but it could prevent you from taking as many breaks during the day, and you might not need as much coffee.

10. Schedule Meetings and Calls in the Afternoon

Because of our natural circadian rhythm, everyone experiences brain fog during the afternoon. Rather than trying to fight it, take a power nap or grab a snack. This might give you the motivation to get through the rest of your day.

Since your energy is not that high during the afternoon, you need to spend your busy work on more challenging and creative work. This means that you only do soft tasks like attending meetings or returning calls. People have realized that three in the afternoon is the best time for meetings.

11. The 52/17 Rule

We are not robots. We need breaks during the day to stay fresh and to be able to work at our best. This is why many people are implementing the Pomodoro Technique, which encourages working in short, focused, and productive bursts and then taking a short break. All you need for this is a timer. It gives you the chance to break big tasks into smaller, more manageable breaks.

This is how it works:

- Pick a task to do
- Set a 25-minute timer
- Work on your chores until the timer goes off
- Take a break for five minutes
- With each session, you will take a longer break

This will help you to accomplish a lot more during the day while still taking breaks. These short time sessions let you focus without getting fatigued mentally.

After Desktop tracked the habits of their employees, they found the average success is working 52 minutes and resting for 17. Even if you do not work for exactly 52 minutes, the main idea here is you need to take breaks to refocus, recharge, and avoid getting burnout.
Despite its simplicity, this technique does have a downside. These sessions are not meant to be interrupted. This is a time to focus. This means you cannot pause in the middle and begin again later. If somebody comes over and asks you to do something, you will need to decline or stop your session. It is possible to get a lot done in just a few sessions.

12. Do Theme Days

The CEO of Square and Twitter, Jack Dorsey, spends eight hours each day at his companies. How is he productive?
He is extremely practiced and disciplined. On Mondays at each company, he focuses on running the company and management. They have a directional meeting at Square and an OpCom meeting at Twitter. He does all the one-on-one management that day.
He focuses on the product on Tuesdays. He focuses on growth, communications, and marketing on Wednesday. He focuses on partnerships and developers on Thursday, and he focuses on recruiting and the culture of the company on Friday.
On Saturday, he hikes. Sundays are used to plan and reflect for the next week. The main reason theme days are effective is they keep him focused. If he gets interrupted, he can deal with the problem quickly and be able to jump into what he was previously working on.

13. Don't Make Decisions

If you have ever wondered why Steve Jobs, Barack Obama, and Mark Zuckerberg always wear the same outfits, it is not because they have no fashion sense or are lazy—they were just reserving their mental energy.
As our day wears on, our ability to make good decisions will decrease. When we do not have to make a decision, we are preventing what is known as decision fatigue.

People who are productive stay away from decision fatigue by streamlining and automating as many decisions as possible. This might be laying out your clothes the day before, prepping your meals on Sunday, and using software to schedule meetings.

14. Flexible Routines

Scheduling will keep you organized and focused, but you do not want to block out every single minute of your day. This is why successful and productive people try to schedule some white space in their calendars. When you start scheduling in white spaces, you will see a brand new you.

This when you take the time to catch your breath, meditate, or reflect. You might be thinking that you do not have time to just sit and do nothing. An easy way around this is when you schedule a meeting that you know will last about thirty minutes, block out forty instead. This way you have ten minutes either before or after your meeting to do whatever you want.

A different option is to keep an entire day open. Tim Ferriss will not plan any activities on Mondays or Fridays. He even tells his assistants not to take phone calls on Mondays or Fridays just in case he wants to take a long weekend. He always uses Mondays for prioritizing and preparing for his week, or for any administrative tasks he must handle.

He does not have anything on the schedule, so he gets to choose what to do. None of the obligations are unpleasant or financially driven. If he gets the chance to do something fun that comes up at the last minute, he can cancel everything in a moment's notice.

15. Relax Each Evening

Because productive people have fulfilling but busy lives, they usually take off every evening. Why? They get the chance to recharge and be ready for the next day. What do they do when they are not working? They do what they like to do and relax and reduce their stress. Then they get ready for bed and get between six and eight hours of sleep.

16. Polyphasic Sleep

This method will sound a bit bizarre and will likely only work for a few people. If you find that it works for you, then you will notice a lot more productivity during your day.

Most people are what is known as monophasic sleepers. This simply means you get all your sleep in during the night in about an eight-hour chunk. People who sleep in two small chunks like four hours during the morning and four hours during the evening are biphasic sleepers. People who are polyphasic sleepers take this method to the extreme. They break their sleep cycles into several phases that will have less sleep but improves productivity. How much sleep you get in each phase could vary. Some people might take just a twenty-minute nap where others need a larger chunk and then supplement with more naps.

A Russian project manager has started using this method where he sleeps for 3.5 hours each night and then takes twenty-minute naps three times a day. Because of this, he says he has a lot more work time and can get more done than he normally would. His largest benefit is he gets two months of free time every year.

Polyphasic sleep can help you feel alert and healthy. It can give you sleep that is more satisfying and can help increase your productivity. This scheduling does have some drawbacks. It is a challenge to live with this type of sleep schedule while also managing regular family life. If you end up missing your sleep sessions, it might throw you off-balance.

There are plenty of advantages to this method, like having more working hours during the day. For a person who only sleeps for four hours, they will have twenty-eight extra hours each week to work.

17. Find the Right Mix

To find your most productive schedule, you might have to create a hybrid of these options. This method works very well with time blocking. You can fit three Pomodoro sessions into a ninety-minute work session. You might be on your own with the polyphasic method.

You must schedule your day. If you do not, somebody else will. When you set a daily schedule, you will make sure that you are the person prioritizing your life.

Structuring Your Day for Maximum Productivity

If you have been following a routine and have become tired of it, it is time to shake things up. There are various ways you can set yourself up for daily success. Whether you write down your list or use a computer, there are many options for switching things up. Just experiment with a few and see what will work for you.

Here are some things you can do to help structure your day to keep things interesting:

- If you work freelance and get to choose the hours you work, you are a lucky person. You get to do whatever you would like as long as you get your work turned in on time.

- Do not try to change your routine overnight. You would be better off making small, simple changes.

- If you are looking for fulfillment and productivity, try simple things like working on one goal every day to help boost your motivation.

- An ultimate routine will not stop at the office: it takes into account rest, exercise, and nutrition.

- Try motivating yourself by visualizing your tasks rather than typing them or writing them down.

- If you want your morning to be more productive, ditch your emails and do something exciting first.

- The most common strategy involves structuring your day by time. This means figuring out whether evening, afternoon, or morning is more productive for you. Once you find it, stick with it.

- If you are not ready to let go of your normal routine, begin with something small like organizing your to-do list differently to see what will work best for you.

Planning Your Day
Here are some steps I take to plan my day:

- Write down everything you have to do.

You can use an app, pen and paper, journal, or whatever feels right for you. Write down EVERY SINGLE THING that you have to do. You can work off your weekly plan for this, but you might add more things that will happen during the week while planning your daily process.
An example of what a typical day might look like:

  o Morning routine

  o Exercise

  o Read for 30 minutes

  o Eat no more than 2500 calories today

  o Take a walk

  o Write a blog

  o Publish a blog

  o Interview new applicants

  o Get in touch with the contractor for a quote

  o Call mom

  o Plan a date with friends

  o Send thank-you notes

  o Go to yoga class

These are the things I want to get done for the day. You might notice that they are scattered and it is not an organized list. This might work for some, but the main thing is it must work for you. If you have to write things down in the order they need to be done, then that is how you make your list.

- You must know what your outcome will be.

What do you want? This is the most important question you must ask yourself. You might want to exercise today, but do you just want to exercise to say that you did? The reason for the exercise needs to accomplish a certain goal or outcome. Most people exercise to build muscle while maintaining energy and staying healthy.
This is why you need to know what your outcome or goal is. Here is something that I would write for my outcome: "I am going to make progress toward the new merger with the new company." That is my outcome. That is the goal I am working toward. Now that you know your goal, you can figure out some other activities that could help you achieve that.

- Know the purpose and why you want it.

When you have figured out what you want and have it written in your journal, now you must write the reasons why you want it. Write underneath your goals why you want this to happen. You could just write down a few bullet points if you are in a hurry.
These reasons are what will motivate you and give you the fuel to reach your goal. Try to make your reasons quick so you do not take too much time on this and ruin your morning. While you are writing these things down, you might begin to feel motivated to start your day and excited to take action.

- Create a plan of action

When you know what you want and the reasons you want it, now you need to make an action plan. This is when you take everything you have written down and organize them for each of your goals.

Let's say you are going to concentrate on your exercise routine today. This is how you might organize your day:

- Go to the gym
- Work my arms
- Only eat 2500 calories today
- Go to yoga class
- Take a walk
- Make and drink a healthy drink
- Walk the dog around the block before bed.

Now that you know your goal, you can add more items that will help you reach your goal better and faster.

- More planning and organizing

Doing these things is more effective than a normal "to-do" list. It is creating a power plan for the day that will motivate and fulfill you once you reach your goal.

To take it one step further, be sure to schedule these actions. You can use a calendar app on your phone to schedule exactly what you need to do and when you need to do it. Schedule everything, including phone calls you need to make during the day.

When you make a schedule, you will know exactly when things are going to happen. Do not leave anything to "whenever I have the time" because we all know that your time can be taken over in a second by other things.

- Use leverage

Think about ways you could outsource and leverage things to others if possible. It is all about working smarter and not harder. You may be able to hire freelancers or assistants to help you reach your goals faster. This can make your life a lot easier. You will be able to focus on the most important things that you are best at.

Tools and Apps to Help Get You Organized

Between the to-do lists, appointments, activities, and work, most of us feel anxious and rushed. Most of the time, our smartphones are the biggest distraction of all, and this just makes our day more hectic. However, your phone could streamline your life, depending on how you employ it. You can use the following to help you track how you use your time, get reminders, and create better habits. Here is how your phone can be turned into a timesaver:

1. Pocket

The internet rabbit hole is one of the biggest timewasters out there. When you see a story that seems interesting, do not read it right away. Rather, use Pocket to save it and then go back to it when you have more time.

Pocket gives you the chance to save articles while browsing through sites. You can organize the videos and articles you have collected into categories that allow you to find them easily when you want them. When you have saved some things into Pocket, the app will begin recommending articles that you might be interested in.

By using this app, you might catch up on your reading if you find yourself without an internet connection. Pocket can cache the articles so you can read them offline. If you have the app on several devices, it will sync them all up.

2. Habit List

Their tagline is: "build a better you," and this app will help you with that. It will help you to make better choices, like regularly going through your paperwork.

To use the app, just write down some achievements on the calendar or schedule some recurring habits. This app will then remind you about the tasks you need to complete. It will also give you a progress report to see how this is going. Its interface is simple and helps you stay focused. Each morning, it will display a list of your day's tasks. To create several different habits, you will have to pay $5. Even though Habit List is only applicable for iOS, Android users have a similar app they can use known as Habit Streak.

3. Todoist

This is the most popular app for the to-do list. This tool works with every platform, it has an intuitive and bright interface, and, for those who need them, there are advanced features.

This will give you the chance to prioritize different tasks. You could arrange tasks by putting them with each other and this, in turn, allows you to keep your personal and work items separate. For tasks that occur often, such as paying bills, you can set these to replay regularly. If you have tasks each week, Todoist will not forget.

You can use this app for free, but you can upgrade to a premium plan for only $29 a year. With the upgrade, you can request reminders based on where you are and the time, automatic backups, and charts that will show you your achievements.

4. Smarter Time

If you want to get your life better organized, you must know how you are spending your time. This app tries to help you do just that. It can automatically track your activities. You will need to chart your time yourself, but the app will also try to fill in any gap that you have during the day by using your previous habits that it gets from your phone's sensors. Fast movements could mean that you took a run during the morning.

When you begin feeding this app some data, it will generate reports on all sorts of things from the way you use your time to the apps spend your time on. If you are looking to change things up, you can create custom goals that Smarter Time will help you achieve.

This app is only available for Android users, but they are working on a beta version for iOS. For a more accurate report or more data, you can upgrade to a plus account that will cost between $3 and $10 every month.

5. Trello

This app has gained great fame as a tool that teams use to guide shared projects. It works great for families and individuals because its appeal is how flexible the app is. It can be adapted for several things, including keeping track of various goals.

You can use both web and mobile apps, and they both work the same way. You create various "cards" and place them into columns. Every card could symbolize a chore, a task on your to-do list, or a big holiday that is coming up. These columns could represent many dates, levels or priority, tasks, or other factors you may employ to get your cards in order.

When you have determined how you are going to organize your cards, you can add designs to each card to make them easy to maintain. You could apply a colored label, a summary, tag people who might need to be reminded, or give task deadlines. Then you will collaborate and add comments, attach files, and move cards from column to column. The setup can range from simple to very complex.

To be used personally, you can take advantage of its free tier. Businesses can pay between $10 and $21 each month to have better integration with other apps you may use.

6. Cortana

These days, most phones will come with a digital helper. While most people turn to Siri or Google Assistant, Cortana might be helpful, especially if you work on many gadgets or you have a Windows 10 computer. All you have to do is download the app. Then you will sign in to your Microsoft account and allow her to systematize your life.

Cortana can set tasks reminders, create lists, and take notes. When a reminder is set, it will ping you at different times of the day or when you get to a specific location. You could get an alert to buy your partner flowers when you pass by your favorite flower shop. You can place reminders on a schedule to repeat so you can make a weekly reminder.

Cortana will work with any calendar, including those from Microsoft, Apple, and Google, that allows you to add new events and review for appointments. Cortana can keep you in the loop about weather forecasts and breaking news.

7. Google Keep

To start, you will neat an app that takes notes where you could put all your fragmented notes, lists, and scribbles. Google Keep has a straightforward interface and is compatible with many platforms.

In addition to storing notes, Google Keep will give you many ways to organize them. You could label related entries by using the same tag or color. This makes it easier to group them together like things that are related to "children," "work," or "home." It can store lists that have checkboxes, scribbles that have been drawn with a finger or stylus, images, and voice memos.

You could share Google Keep notes with other people who use it and put them into a more professional format by converting them into a Google Docs file.

Celebrate the Day

While you are taking action and checking off all those things you have accomplished, be sure to celebrate your progress. The more you acknowledge yourself and your accomplishments, the more productive you will be. You will feel more successful in taking action, and this is what you want.

What if you didn't get everything on your list done? It is fine. It might be humanly impossible to get everything done in a day's time. Your main goal is to be sure you reach your most important goal, not every one of them.

Move anything you haven't done to the top of the list for tomorrow. As long as you get the most important tasks done, then your day has been a success. You need to focus on making progress and stop trying to be perfect. This is what works for me when I plan my day.

As you can see, there are many philosophies and methods out there. This is why it is important for you to try different things until you find the one that works best for you.

Get Your Lifestyle Right

You might have a huge presentation to give at work the next day, or you might be running a marathon. Your family and friends will all tell you that you need to "get a good night's sleep." We say things like this because we all know it is important to get sleep to perform well. For some unknown reason, everyone is trying to find out how to do more with less sleep.

This is the total opposite of what we need to do. To be more productive, sleep is a big player. Let us find out how not sleeping well will hurt productivity and getting good sleep will improve it. Let us see how you can make sure the sleep you are getting is productive too.

How Sleep Affects Productivity

Almost half of all Americans have reported that insufficient or low-quality sleep has interfered with their lives at least once a week. It seems like we already know that getting inadequate sleep will impact our productivity negatively. With increased work hours, the more tired people feel, the more they will make mistakes. We will be sluggish or procrastinate, and this will block our creativity.

Researchers realized these effects during the late 1800s when it was recommended dropping the workday from nine hours to eight hours, for a total of forty hours each week. They noticed that after that amount of time, the worker's output was significantly reduced.

Most people work more than forty hours, and if you are working a sensible number of hours but not getting good sleep, your work may not be productive. When I say "good sleep," I am referring to the consistency and amount of sleep.

- Insufficient Sleep

Insufficient sleep is the number-one productivity killer. If you do not get the right amount of sleep, your productivity will suffer. You won't have a lot of energy and your reaction time will be slower. You won't be as focused and will be less creative. You will have a hard time solving problems and making decisions. Sleep deprivation causes these effects, and you might also see them in some coworkers.

One study done in 2010 watched 4,000 workers at four different corporations in America. The workers who claimed they did not get good sleep or who suffered from insomnia had the most productivity losses. They spent about three times longer just trying to manage their time.

The workers who were deprived of sleep did not make good decisions, had a hard time remembering things, problems focusing, and were not as motivated. Sleep deprivation can devastate us emotionally, physically, and mentally. If we do not get the right amount of sleep, we will have problems focusing throughout the day. If we do learn something new, it will not stick with us. Our brain will consolidate memories in REM sleep, but REM sleep normally takes part during the last part of the night. If we do not sleep enough, we will be missing out on REM sleep.

We will also miss deep sleep time. This is a sleep stage that is responsible for repairing and restoring our body tissue and muscles. Because of this, our muscles will hurt more and we will get tired faster. A study discovered that athletes who did not sleep well got tired 11 percent faster than athletes who slept well. Chronic sleep deprivation has been linked with many health problems like cardiovascular disease, type 2 diabetes, and obesity.

You can easily see how sleep deprivation can negatively affect your productivity levels in life, work, and school. The effects of sleep deprivation are similar to someone who is drunk. Most people know just how unproductive a person is when they are intoxicated. If you try to do an all-nighter, your response time will be 50 percent slower than a person who has a blood-alcohol level of 0.1 percent.

- Inconsistent Sleep

The next part of making sure you get good sleep it to get consistent sleep. A 2017 study followed some undergrad students. They wore actigraphy wristbands that monitored their sleeping schedules before they were given cognitive assessments. If their sleep schedules were very irregular, they did a lot worse on their cognitive tests. These findings are consistent with what other researchers have found. They all suggest that sleep regularity is as important as how much sleep you get.

One research team in 2017 watched Harvard college students for one month and compared their academic performance to their sleep patterns. Every one of the students got the same amount of sleep, but the ones who kept a regular sleep schedule did better than the ones who did not. The students who would wake up and go to bed at different times had delayed circadian rhythms and lower grades. The melatonin in these students was released later than the ones who kept a consistent sleep cycle. They experienced what is known as jet lag even though they had not traveled.

This study proved why keeping a consistent sleep cycle is an important part of productivity. The circadian rhythm dictates our sleep cycle. This is our day-to-night cycle. According to that schedule, our bodies will release melatonin each evening to signal our brain to begin falling asleep. Each morning, our cortisol levels begin to rise as our melatonin levels get lower. This helps wake up the body and gets us ready for our day. If we do not make sure that we keep a normal sleep cycle, the production of melatonin will be delayed, and this keeps us from falling asleep at the right time. We will begin to experience a trickle-down effect on the rest of our body's functions.

If you ignore your internal body clock, it could have serious effects on productivity. A good example of this would be people who work at night and have schedules that are flipped. Every study that has been done shows that people will have performance problems that could range from work errors that cause a loss in productivity, impaired focus, and more significant problems such as driving while sleepy.

- Cost of Productivity

Productivity losses do cost actual money. The RAND Corporation did a study during 2016 and realized that sleep deprivation cost the economy in the United States about $411 billion each year and over one million workdays were lost. People showed up late or overslept, they even skipped work completely because of illnesses they were susceptible to since they were not getting the right amount of sleep. If they were able to go to work, they were not as productive and focused. On a personal level, this translates to about eleven days of lost productivity and around $2,200 of lost wages every year.

Regardless of your job, mistakes are bad, but they are very serious for people who work in specific industries such as the medical field. Researchers estimated that medical errors might have been lowered by a third just by making their work shifts shorter and letting people get a little extra sleep.

Increase Productivity with Better Sleep

It is good news that the relationship between productivity and sleep works in both directions. Since poor sleep makes productivity worse, good sleep will make it better.

If you can get the right amount of sleep, you will enjoy the following benefits:

- Lower risk of burnout
- More accuracy and fewer errors
- Easy problem solving
- Better creative flow
- Better memory
- Better decision-making skills and judgment
- Better reaction times

You must get the right amount of sleep to enjoy these benefits. Even if you get a lot of sleep, you won't get any benefits if the sleep is not deep. People who have allergic rhinitis are at risk because this can cause nasal congestion that will hinder their ability to breathe while sleeping. This causes them to experience poor sleep along with less productivity at work or school.

Some studies have been done about all the improvement with students who got to attend a school that had a later start time. When they reach puberty, teens have a shift in their circadian rhythm that will change their need to go to sleep one hour later each evening. The problem with this is that it coincides with having to go to school earlier and have the rest of their day filled with homework and other activities. Many sleep experts across the nation are trying to get schools to begin their day one hour earlier because they found that an extra hour could improve test scores.

Getting good sleep simply means that you can think better. People like Dali, Einstein, and Larry Page have stated that they get their best ideas during sleep. Getting a good amount of REM sleep can stimulate your creative juices. This explains why you can wake up with solutions to problems you have been trying to solve or with brilliant new ideas.

Making Sleep Productive

If you are looking to make your sleep productive, you must make sure that you get good sleep. The following are some tips on how you can be a more productive sleeper:

- Figure Out Your Sleep Schedule

What schedule works best for productivity? This will depend on your chronotype, which is just a fancy way of saying that you are either an early bird or a night owl; your chronotype controls your internal clock. This tells you whether you are going to be productive in the mornings or at night. Rather than making your chronotype fit into society standards, learn what it is and try to work with it.

Other than your chronotype, you should make sure that you get enough sleep so that you feel rested. For a normal adult, between seven to seven and a half hours is recommended each night. The right amount for you could be out of this range. If you get up after just sleeping six hours and you feel great, do not force yourself to sleep another hour. If you do not feel great until after eight hours of sleep, accept it and make room to sleep eight hours.

When you know the amount of sleep you need, create a schedule that lets you sleep that long and follow it no matter what. If you can train your body on a normal sleep schedule, it will be easier for you to go to sleep and get up. This schedule must be followed every day, as well as weekends, so that your sleep debt does not build up.

- Calm Routine

Every night in the last thirty minutes before you go to bed, do the same activities in the exact same order. It is normally one hour but because most people have busy schedules, we have shortened it to thirty.

Your goal here is to train your brain by associating your bedtime routine as getting ready to go to sleep. Try to do the same calm activities if you can. Have a cup of "sleepy" tea, make a to-do list, and take a warm bath. If you write down your tasks, it will get them out of your mind so you can deal with them tomorrow rather than lying awake worrying about them.

- Calm Environment

Make sure you only use your bed for sex and sleep. Do not use it for watching television, hobbies, or work. You need to associate your bed with relaxation and rest, not anything that might excite you or cause stress like television or work.

Other than these things, there are many things you can do to make your bedroom more conducive for sleep. Keep it dark and cool. Set the temperature in the middle 60s and use an eye mask or blackout curtains if you need them. Make sure you have a good mattress and that your bedding is comfortable. Keep your bedroom clean to prevent irritations and allergies. Keep it free from clutter to help relax your mind.

- No Phones

Any electronic device will interfere with sleep. If you are like many, your smartphone will be your largest hindrance for getting the proper sleep. The main problem with looking at your electronic devices before going to sleep is that they give off a strong blue wavelength. The brain perceives this wavelength as sunlight.

The more of this your eyes take in, the more your brain will believe it is daytime and that you need to be awake and alert. We have a tendency to hold our electronics closer to our face, and this really drowns your eyes with that blue light. Most of the time, we are reading emails and checking social media, and both can activate stressors.

- Power Naps

Everybody needs a break occasionally. The best way to get it is to take a nap.

A simple definition of a power nap is just a quick nap that only lasts twenty to thirty minutes to help boost productivity. The shortness of the nap is why it is so refreshing, and this is why you must keep it short. If you go over thirty minutes, you will risk getting into a deep sleep, it will be harder to wake up, and you will feel worse.

It is important to take the nap when you feel you need it the most. This usually will be around two or three in the afternoon. Make sure you schedule this break, make a note in your calendar, and then find a nice quiet place where nobody will judge or disturb you. To take this to another level, have some coffee right before you take your nap, then you will wake up feeling alert.

- Sunshine

Sunshine will wake you up. You might wonder how getting more sunshine will help you sleep better? If your body gets plenty of natural sunlight, especially during the early morning hours, it will help to synchronize your circadian cycle. This will help keep your brain alert and awake during the day when the sun is out, and it will be ready to go to sleep when the sun goes down.

Get an extra boost by getting that morning sun while having a brisk walk or engaging in other outside activities. You can also use what is known as a light therapy box. This can be kept on your desk during the morning, or, better yet, move your desk to a nearby window.

- Exercise

Exercise is another activity that will energize you and will help you sleep better. It all depends on when you do the exercise. Do not exercise at night because it will wake up your nervous system and make it harder for you to go to sleep. If you exercise early in the day, it will physically tire your body so that when you go to bed, you are ready to go to sleep.

- Be Careful of What You Drink and Eat

Eating a healthy diet will give you a healthy body along with some healthy sleep. Eat healthy during the day but be careful of what you eat in the afternoon. Do not ingest any alcohol, drugs, or caffeine. Be careful about heavy dinners that are full of fatty foods or having sugary snacks late at night. All these things will mess up your mind and digestive systems. This interferes with your ability to go to sleep and remain asleep. If you do have some alcohol, it might help you fall asleep to begin with, but it will just interrupt your sleep and you will wake up earlier.

- Wake Up the Right Way

Finish up your productive sleep by waking up productively too. Never hit the snooze button. Jump out of bed and begin your morning routine. This might include a few pushups, jumping jacks, a brisk walk, making some coffee, and brushing your teeth. Open a window and let in the sun or use an alarm clock that simulates the sun.

Do not look at your emails or phone immediately to let your body adjust to the new day before you let yourself be hit with more stress.

- Create Tasks While Sleeping

If you are worried about not getting all your tasks done by sleeping all the time, think about how you could schedule specific tasks to happen while you are asleep.

Get tomorrow's dinner cooked by using a slow cooker. Travel for business using red-eyes so you will be able to sleep during the flight. If there is something that you need to solve, or you have to take a test the following day, glance at the material right before you head to bed so that your mind will be focused on it while you are sleeping.

How Sleep Can Help Your Career

As stated above, getting the perfect amount of sleep will not just boost your mood and fill your body with loads of energy, it could help your boss notice you and you might even get that promotion. Still need some convincing? Look at how getting the right amount of sleep can improve your performance on the job.

- Won't Be Distracted

If you are deprived of sleep, you will have problems focusing on your tasks after you have been disrupted. Compare this to somebody who gets plenty of sleep. Being refreshed comes in handy if you have a cubicle mate who likes to chitchat or children who want to turn on the television when you go into your office if you work from home.

- Prevent Burnout

If you sleep less than six hours every night, this is the number one cause of burnout on the job. Sleep deprivation can cost you a lot of money in lost productivity. You need to adopt the habit of getting better sleep now so you can raise the odds of enjoying your job and staying in your career for many years to come.

- Improved Memory

Getting the right amount of sleep is the main component for turning what you learn into concrete thoughts. If you do not get enough sleep, chances of poor memory increase compared to people who get the right amount of sleep.

- Better Decisions

Getting the correct amount of sleep will improve your ability to make quick decisions by 4 percent. It might not sound like much, but every bit will help.

- Fewer Mistakes

Even if you are just slightly sleep-deprived, your response time will be 50 percent slower on easy tasks than a person who is drunk.

To Sum Up Sleep and Productivity

- Sleep deprivation is the main killer of performance.

- A link has been found between drowsy driving, accidents at work, and sleep deprivation. Not getting enough sleep will affect how the brain performs and normally results in bad cognitive performance.

- Find out your chronotype. Figure out the best time for you to sleep and work so your body can adjust to your schedule to help your productivity instead of holding it back.

- If you have a job where you are creative, or you just want to be more creative, getting better REM sleep will allow you to turn your dreams into creative endeavors.

- Sleep can affect all aspects of productivity, even physically. Athletes can learn how better sleep can to improve their work performance and make them a more successful competitor.

- Productivity losses are an economic problem.

- Despite what most workaholics think, this is a big obstacle to their productivity and sleep.

- Create a perfect sleep environment that includes pleasant smells, colors, and lighting.

Productivity and Nutrition

You have probably heard the old saying: "You are what you eat!" Even though there is some truth to this quote, most people have not considered how deep this logic applies to the important aspects of our lives.

Whilst it is true that we are what we eat, it is also true that we work how we eat. This means diet impacts productivity levels more than we realize. Everyone knows it is important to eat well to keep our bodies healthy. What you might not know is it is equally important for your mind. Healthy diets do not just help you lower your cholesterol and control your weight; they can improve your productivity, problem-solving skills, alertness, and concentration.

It is no secret that our digestive system uses energy to do its job. Our bodies only have so much energy for everything, which is why we must watch what we eat when we are trying to get the best performance from our body and mind. Eating too much of the wrong foods throughout the day could seriously impair our productivity.

What is the link between increased productivity and the right nutrition? You can look at it in numbers. The Centers for Disease Control says that about 1/3 of all American adults are overweight. These increasing rates can lead to heart disease and diabetes along with more cost for the workplace because of decreased productivity.

This link between productivity and bad nutrition goes beyond obesity. Let us find out how nutrition can change your productivity and figure out ways to improve both parts of your life.

Consequences of a Bad Diet

The main idea behind "you are what you eat" is everything we eat will affect the way our body performs. If we eat healthy foods, our body will process the nutrients and then use them for the best energy possible. Bad nutrition will not give us the energy we need. Our overall well-being and productivity will suffer as a result.

A different way to understand this link is to look at how bad nutrition can affect your workday. Bad eating habits could lead to:

- Decreased productivity
- High levels of depression and stress
- Inability to do our jobs effectively
- Inability to think clearly
- Low levels of energy
- Irritability
- Decreased mental capacity
- Fatigue

Dietary Habits and Sleep Cycles

As previously stated, our bodies are controlled by our circadian rhythms. These tell us when we are tired, need sleep, and feel alert.

Various things can mess up these rhythms. You have probably experienced this in the form of jet lag if you fly a lot. Most people do not realize that our eating habits are the main culprit. How we eat could seriously harm our circadian rhythms, and this can cause you to feel tired at times when you should not feel tired.

Our body views eating as more important than sleep and this is why what you eat has a large effect on your sleep cycle. Our bodies have an internal clock. The more we bring our diets in line with it, the more likely we will be to harness all our potential during the day. You should not eat too much in the evenings, stay away from fatty foods if you have a large mental load, and be sure to eat your biggest meal in the mornings.

Our diets have a huge impact on productivity, even more than we even realize. Eating incorrect foods at the wrong time of day could throw a wrench in our workday. If you pay attention, it becomes easier to turn food into fuel for your body and, thus, use it to help you get through your day and get the most out of it.

Low Self-Control Is Caused by Low Blood Sugar

Most people do not know that self-control and productivity go hand in hand. Our capacity to remain focused on a task is connected to willpower, and it is believed that our ability to stay away from temptation is linked to our glucose levels.

Glucose is a fancy word for blood sugar. Everyone knows that low blood sugar happens when we do not eat food at the right times, and it can have adverse effects on our behaviors and moods. One study states, "Glucose gives us energy for most of our brain's activities, and it is plausible that self-control, as a particularly expensive process in terms of complex brain activity, is especially dependent on glucose." Basically, this is saying that low blood sugar can cause a reduction in willpower, and you will find it hard to stay on track and do your best work.

Carbohydrates Kill Productivity

Carbohydrates have become a bad thing over the past few years, and there is a good reason for this. While they are a necessary part of a healthy diet, they are not the most important part of your meals. Eating too many carbs can kill productivity.

Carbs can be found in foods that are sugar and grain oriented. Because they are closely related, our body's insulin levels could negatively affect our energy reserves. Foods that are full of carbs can cause our bodies to produce more insulin, which fills our brain with tryptophan and serotonin. Serotonin is mostly stored in the gut. This might make the association between energy levels and diet a bit more explicit.

Productivity and Physical Health

Obesity rates have been strongly linked to the sedentary lifestyle that most Americans have these days. Obesity can also be caused by poor nutrition thanks to the large amounts of empty calories found in high-fat, high-carb processed foods.

How does poor nutrition link obesity with productivity? Research shows that people who have been diagnosed as obese are likely to experience sleep apnea and insomnia. These could cause fatigue during the day, which can zap your energy and, in turn, your productivity.

Obesity can carry the risk of many health consequences. Fatigue is only one side effect of obesity. It could lead to more bad food choices and even more decreased productivity. Improving your nutrition can help you stop this cycle.

- Cognition and Nutrition

Energy level is not the only thing affected by bad nutrition. You might experience some irritability when you eat processed foods. With time, bad nutrition can increase the risk of anxiety and depression. If you have already been diagnosed with mental health problems, you might experience other symptoms when you do not eat right. Depression and anxiety can make it hard to concentrate while at work. In severe cases, it can be hard to just get out of bed each morning.

Nutrition does not just affect our energy levels and mood. It can impact our creativity. Knowing this could be very helpful if you have to be creative at your job.

People usually associate eating right with managing their weight, but eating right is necessary to nourish our brain. Think about increasing the intake of these nutrients to help your productivity levels and improve your brain health:

- o Vitamin E, found in vegetable oils and nuts
- o Vitamin C, found in citrus fruits, bell peppers, and berries
- o Omega-3 fatty acids, found in certain eggs, walnuts, flaxseed, and fish
- o Folate, found in greens, beans, and meat

Remember to drink a lot of water during the day. Some studies have found that dehydration can cause bad planning skills. Having a cup of coffee each morning is fine, just be sure to cut back in the evening so you do not overstimulate your brain close to bedtime.

- Effects at Work

Many people think about productivity as being a personal thing, but nutrition plays a large role in global productivity. Several studies have shown that workers who are in poor health are the main cause of decreased productivity across the world. Malnutrition could impact how adults work in nations that are developing, and obesity and other health problems could influence people who live in countries that are already developed. Adults in good health might be able to work longer hours and reach higher incomes during their lifetime.

Tips for Increased Productivity and Better Nutrition

There are ways you can stay away from all these negative outcomes and make sure your productivity remains high all day. Try these tips:

- Healthy Breakfast

In order to have a productive day, you must start before you leave your house by having a nutritious breakfast. You must begin your day by having your body fueled and ready to go. It is important to use the correct type of fuel to make sure you have steady energy so you can concentrate during the day. Do not just reach for a doughnut. This will hurt you more than it will help. Try to stick to these food groups:

　　o Low-fat dairy: Low-fat cheese, yogurt, and skim milk

　　o Low-fat protein: Tofu, hemp seeds, nuts, plant proteins, lean meats, peanut butter, and hard-boiled eggs.

　　o Whole grains: Melba toast, bran muffins, bagels, rolls, crackers, and cereals.

　　o Vegetables and fruits: Fresh is always best but you can eat frozen. You can have smoothies or juices. Just be sure the label states 100 percent fruit juice.

- Never Skip a Meal

If you are very busy at work, it is easy to skip a meal to try to be more productive. Don't do this! When you skip meals, it will hurt you later in the day in the form of decreased energy, and this, in turn, hurts our productivity levels. When the body does not have a regular supply of food during the day, it won't get the protein, minerals, and vitamins it needs to function.

You might think skipping meals will help your waistline, but it won't. Our bodies will compensate for these missed meals, which could lead to fat increasing and muscles decreasing.

- Plan Ahead and Pack Your Lunch

To stay away from the temptation to skip meals, going to the vending machine, or going with coworkers to the fast-food joint around the corner, you need to pack your lunch to make sure you have the food you need. Fixing a sandwich on wraps, pits, or whole grain bread are all good choices, especially when you pair them with lean meats, sliced eggs, tuna, or hummus. Salads are great to pack too, as long as you keep the dressing separate from the greens. Pack small containers of apples, bananas, granola bars, almonds, and chopped vegetables to snack on throughout the day to keep your body and brain humming.

The choices you make at lunch could impact your productivity for the rest of the day. Eating a fast food meal that is high in fats will only give you empty calories and can cause a spike in your blood glucose, which will cause you to crash later. You will probably experience these slumps on days when you eat fast food rather than on the days you pack your own lunch.

You also need to plan ahead. Do not try to figure out what to eat for lunch when you take your break, and do not grab snacks in the breakroom. Planning your snacks and meals beforehand will give you enough energy to help you make it through your day. This can help you resist the temptation of grabbing a quick, processed meal.

- Nutrition Should Be a Priority

Talk with your bosses and coworkers about how you can make the workplace more nutritional. As a group, find ways to bring nutritious foods into the workplace that will improve productivity, well-being, and morale. Initiatives in workplace nutrition could increase productivity by about 2 percent.

Eating healthy can give you many benefits that last a lifetime. If you do not eat healthily, try to make some changes. It is not reasonable to expect a change overnight. If you make a huge change too quickly, it might decrease the likelihood that you will stick with it.

Slowly changing your nutritional changes is the key to having success in the long run. You will notice small changes in your productivity levels.

Track Your Time

There might have been times when you have gotten to the end of your day and wonder where your time went. Most of the items on your to-do list haven't been done, but you spent eight hours doing...what?

Everybody would like to improve their productivity, both in their personal lives and in business. What exactly does it mean to measure and track productivity, and how can it be done? Before we go further, let us first look at what productivity is: "productivity is the state of being able to create or generate services and goods."

Once you get to work, how much time do you spend getting your coffee? How long does your computer take to boot up? Once your computer is up and running, how long do you spend looking through the emails from yesterday? How long does it take before you start your work for the day?

Workers have admitted that they waste about three hours each day on tasks that are not work-related. You might be thinking that is not you. Whether you do it intentionally or not, if you were to track your tasks and time every day, the results might surprise you.

Think about productivity when you are mindlessly scrolling through social media. Can you create something from that? If you are networking while on Facebook, then you are being productive. If you are only scrolling without doing or creating anything, then this is not being productive.

With the increasing usage of software as a service, or SaaS, along with the numerous applications available for every smartphone, it is very easy for anybody, especially employers, to track people while at work or in the field when they are on the clock. The reason behind the need for this technology comes from people having a hard time distinguishing between their personal life and work.

The socialization on social media platforms via smartphones has brought into question how much impact this has had on productivity. One side of the debate, distractions are known to limit productivity. The other side says that workplace controls such as shutting down social media usage and internet access could cause problems with happiness in the workplace. This can cause a challenge for many employers who like to keep track of productivity and their employees without inhibiting or limiting their freedoms.

The Hawthorne effect shows that people will change their behaviors like performing better and working harder because they realize they are being watched.

One such app is called RescueTime, which makes it easy to see where your hours and minutes went. Once you have downloaded the app, it will begin to track your time immediately. It will categorize various applications and sites based on how productive or distracting they are. You can customize these in the settings. It will then display this data on a dashboard where you will be able to see how your days, weeks, and months were spent.

Most services make you input all your activities yourself, which is very time consuming, but RescueTime will do all this for you. It will not just track what websites you visit but other applications you use too. The number of hours you spend working on or editing your work will count toward your productivity time.

You do not even need to remember to check the app to see how you have done. It will send you a weekly email to show you your productivity from the prior week. It will give you the perfect snapshot of where your time went and things you can do to improve it. With a premium membership, you can input a set of goals and the app will let you know whether you will meet them by the end of the week.

There are many customizable options like what categories specific activities get put into, the time of day the app needs to track, and activities it needs to ignore. It also has tools that can help you reach better productivity goals by blocking the most distracting websites. This app is a great powerhouse for regaining your time. Basic reporting and tracking are free, but services like getting focused, setting goals, and a dashboard are in the premium package.

Business and Personal Productivity

There are ways that you can measure and track your productivity in both business and personal life. You need to track the time you use for specific tasks, like how much time you spend on social media and how much you get done. This is the only way you can tell if you are being productive. Guesswork will not help. You must use tools to show you how much time specific tasks take. The main point here is not to lie to yourself. If you on social media, write it down. Do this for a week and see what happens. The results might surprise you, but you will see where and when you are less productive so you can begin to change some habits.

- Find Time Drains

You just had a "chat" with a coworker who dropped by to say hi. You "quickly" scanned through your social media pages. You took a "quick" trip to the breakroom to get a bagel or cup of coffee. These might not seem like a problem, but when you combine all these into a dozen or so times every day, these minutes of lost work will add up to reduced productivity.

Do not misunderstand me; everyone needs to take a break during the day. The big problem is losing track of how much time they take up and how many times we do them. You will improve your awareness when you keep a log next to you and record the things you are doing, when you do it, and how long it took. You will then see where those five-minute trips to the break room and that ten-minute "chat" with a coworker derailed your whole day and your workload.

Finding what drains your time and productivity when you are logging your tasks will keep you focused, and this helps you make better decisions and prioritize tasks for the day. This will ultimately help you create procedures to help your day run a lot smoother.

- Tailoring Support and Executive Priorities

When you can track your activities, this will give you and your bosses proof of what you are responsible for. This makes it easy to be on the same page with others you support each day.

Have a conversation with the people you work with to help you work more productively. The conversation might go something like: "Here are my top five priorities. How do these line up with yours? Is there anything on this list that isn't as important as something else?" This will help you develop a laser-like focus that will help you do your job better.

- Putting Tasks Together

I helped coach an administrative assistant some time ago who we will call Sue. She was supposed to be entering business contracts into the company's computer system. There are several steps to this process, and the task required a lot of memory and focus. The problem was that Sue had all sorts of interruptions that came at her from all directions, and soon all those contracts started piling up.

She was getting more and more frustrated and decided to get some help. That is when she called me. I asked Sue to tell me the entire procedure she used for entering these contracts into her system. I wrote them down while she talked. Twenty minutes was how long it took her to remember and do the whole process. I emailed her this process and asked her to print it up and keep it in front of her. I called in a couple of days, and she informed me that, with the steps in front of her, she had cut the time it took her to enter contracts in half.

We did not stop. While we worked on each step together, we figured out that there were natural "batches" that happened during the procedure. Instead of taking every contract through every step individually, we figured out that we could pull all the contracts through every stage together. For example, we filed, tagged, uploaded, and scanned them all at one time and saved a lot more time. Writing down every step and looking for the best way to perform those tasks let Sue clear out the backlog and get back on top of her tasks. When you document and track your tasks each day, and find ways to batch things together, you will be able to achieve better results.

- Strategic Decisions

If you were to count the number of times somebody came by your desk and asked for a "minute" of your time, a favor, or help, how many minutes or hours do you think that would add up to? How many times did you give in to them and then realized too late that your work fell to the side?

When you have a log of your tasks and arrange them in order of priority, it will make it easier to see with a simple glance whether you can agree to their request. If you do not have the time, politely ask them to go to someone else for help, or just say no. Your decision has just become more strategic because you based it on hard data instead of feelings.

- Self-Awareness

It is very easy for a person to simply sit at their desk and daydream. Once the day comes to an end, do you think you will feel like you have accomplished something or did you spend your time putting out fires from the day before? Tracking tasks can help you be more aware of where your time goes.

You cannot get rid of every distraction. Things are always going to come up that need your immediate attention. But when you document what you do, it will let you see where your time has gone.

You can then notice it in advance and be able to redirect yourself before any time has been wasted.

- Online Activity

We all live in a digital world, so you need to know where you spend most of your time online. This can help you figure out if you are being productive. How much time do you spend researching things for work versus scrolling through Facebook? Website tracking tools like the one mentioned above can help you see where you spend the most time so you can begin focusing on areas that will contribute to being more productive.

- Creating Schedules

Tasks won't complete themselves without some planning on your part. The simple task of making a schedule for your goals could help you allot time just for one specific task. If you do get off schedule by starting something different, then you are not being productive. The goal here is to remain on track and get things accomplished.

- Checklists

Have you ever begun your day with a huge to-do list and ended with just a few things checked off? You need to learn to appreciate a simple little checklist. It is a small piece of paper that can help you keep track of your productivity. If you can check off each item or at least more than normal, then you will know that you have been productive for the day.

There are some ways you can keep track of how productive your people are, keep track of them at the workplace and in the field, and keep tabs on your people.

- Work Locations

This may sound a bit counterproductive to boosting efficiency and productivity, but it would be a great idea to allow some of your employees the option to work remotely. If an employee can work where they want to, they can usually focus better and will give you their best work. Many employees will not abuse this perk since they will want to protect that freedom. There are many benefits to letting employees work remotely. These include:

- o Improved communication
- o Feel closer to leaders and management
- o Increased productivity
- o Feel more valued
- o Feel happier when working

You can use any of the tools listed here to track accountability and your people. When a worker can choose where and how they work, it is a great motivator that will increase productivity.

- Ask Your Team for Updates

It is human nature to procrastinate. It is just an attribute that cannot be avoided. You won't have an employee who will give you 100 percent every day, all day long. When you give your employees the freedom to manage their time, this gives them the opportunity to take breaks. You still want to track them to make sure they are doing their work.

Instead of hovering, have them turn in updates at the end of the day. If you have processing software, you can set up alerts as to when progress happens or when approvals are needed. This can help minimize the need for an employee coming to you for your approval in person. It will keep you in the loop to track your people through the day.

One app you could use is called iDoneThis. This simple tool will send reminders to all your team members toward the end of the day. They will reply with an email to tell you about their completed tasks or tasks they are working on. Everybody will receive a team email the next morning. This is a great way to reinforce accountability and improve transparency without having to micromanage your team.

- Micromanaging

Do not get so deep in the data that you are managing every campaign or activity to boost your numbers. Basically, if you stop trying to keep track of people rather than just watching the bottom line, you will still be able to watch productivity while making your team feel valued and them the freedom they need to be creative to help drive growth your mission and vision.

- Get a Bigger Toolbox

Because output is the main thing that counts, begin by communicating your vision, goals, and mission to your workers. Be sure they understand what direction you are going in. From that point, find the right tools to track them and manage their progress. A great tool to use is Tallyfy to set processes and workflow. It can help you to have tools like Asana that will help you track individual tasks along with planning ahead.

- Love Technology

Instead of trying to control productivity by not letting employees use their smartphones, allow them to bring their devices and use them for work. Treat this as an opportunity to invest in your employees. When you let them use their own technology to access process automation apps or project management systems, this could help improve their productivity.

- Track People Using Social Media

"Friending" employees on social media might give you access to their personal lives and it might be more than you would like. It does make it easier to track your employees if you are concerned about them using social media during the time they are at work.

However, if they are getting their work done and finishing all their tasks, then do not stress about social media if they are not breaching any media or confidentiality policies.

- Emphasize Documentation and Communication

For most people, there is a budget for everything. This makes them have to think about customer expectations. They are spending a certain amount of their time on your service or product. It is important that you meet and possibly exceed their expectations.
You can do this by emphasizing documentation and communication with your employees. When you have open communication, it will keep everybody accountable; it allows you to plan for the future and gives you time to take care of problems. It is easier to find people when they are giving you regular updates instead of you having to track them down.

- Trust Your Data

If you do not have every customer interaction and process phase documented and tracked, it can be hard to know which employee did what in landing that major sale or client. For these situations, trust your data and get as much information as you can about the customer. This information needs to include who helped them, what caused them to choose you, and how they heard about the company. The easiest way is to work backward down through the sales funnel. Look at the data to track down the people to figure out which one of your employees was your shining star.

- Quit Measuring Time

When tracking employees, you cannot use time to measure them. You might have two employees who have the exact same set of skills and they give you the same quality of work. One of them might take just a bit longer to finish their task. This is not because they are slacking off; it might be because they are being more thorough. Making an employee speed up could make their quality of work go down.
Rather than trying to track your employees and their work by days, hours, or time, you should measure them by the number of tasks they complete and by their quality of work. Completion of tasks must always be the metric that matters most. This will work even if you break down large tasks into smaller ones to help automation. You

can delegate the components of tasks and measure how well each person produces results against their assigned task.

- Profit Equals Productivity

It is logical to say that profits will always equal productivity. Even small businesses could benefit from measuring their productivity by basing it on profit, since it is very simple and to the point.

- Project Management and Time Tracking Software

Using apps and software that track time and manage projects could help you keep track of productivity in only a few minutes. These do require your employees to electronically submit a copy of their timesheet. You can then use these to check on your team and see how they are doing. Some software will let you run reports based on their performance to see which employees are getting the most sales or taking the time to find more leads.

- Employee Revenue

This can help you find out how productive every employee has been or the amount of revenue that they bring to the company. It is very simple to do; just take the total amount of revenue and divide that by the number of employees you have. The number you come up with will help you figure out what every team member brings or is not bringing to the company.

Basically, if you absolutely must track people by the number of hours they work, there are several apps that let you track activities and time. Basecamp is a project management system. It lets you see when an employee checks items off their task list and when more items were added to a project. By using platforms and applications like these, you can track your people to be sure the right amount of time was spent on tasks. It also lets you know if your team is constantly working during the day.

Streamline Communication

Communication, contrary to popular belief, kills businesses. Small groups of people, or small businesses, tend to do better on the communication front than large groups or business. This is due to the lines of communication.

When there is one person, there are zero lines of communications, but when another person is added, then a single line of communication open up. But when you add one more person, making three people in total, the lines of communication jump to three. This is because of a need to talk to B, and B to C, but C may need to talk to A. The more people you add in, the more lines of communication you will have. Here is how this breaks down:

- Four people, six lines
- Five people, ten lines
- Six people, 15 lines
- Seven people, 21 lines
- Eight people, 28 lines
- Nine people, 36 lines
- Ten people, 45 lines

- Eleven people, 55 lines

- Twelve people, 66 lines

- Thirteen people, 78 lines

- Fourteen people, 91 lines

From four people on, communication starts to get a bit tough because the lines of communication increase exponentially. This is what makes communication for growing businesses so hard because there is no way to tame this.

In theory, if you add an extra person to a project, you should be able to get it done faster. If you add another person to a team, you should be able to move forward at twice the rate. But that is not typically how it works out. Greater inefficiencies happen as more people are added to a team and the lines of communication increase.

Let us say you have a business and one employee, making a total of two people in your business. You two are doing pretty good and getting a lot done and progress well. You decide to add a few more people, thinking your production will increase. Instead, things start to slow down. Why? More people equal more work, right? As we have talked about, more people equal more lines of communication. All those people you have added to your business have to be brought up to speed. The two original workers are the ones who have to bring these subsequent employees up to speed.

So you take one of the two original productive people away from their work to teach a new employee how things work. Once that person, hopefully, learns what to do, they can then start to work on their own. The problem occurs, though, when that person does not work at the same efficiency as their teacher. So now you have somebody working for you who is not as efficient, and it is costing you double.

Many big businesses will face these problems, and they think if people could just communicate more effectively, the problem would go away. Sure, in theory, that is true. But when you are talking about a corporation of one hundred-plus people, it is almost impossible to get everybody on the same page. Even for a company of thirty, it would be hard. To make sure everybody is on the same page, everybody would spend their day telling everybody what they are doing, which is not efficient at all. The exponential cost of communication causes many businesses to die.

So what can be done about this?

Information Architecture

This best way to handle this is through information architecture (IA). IA is made up of three things; people, content, and context. People are the individuals who work for the company, how they come together to create teams, the whole organization, and the physical environment. Context is the vision of the business, its mission, and goals. Once a person is working within a business, and they learn about the context of said business, they will need content. Content can come from communication, data, and feedback.

Everything starts with context. If you do not know what the business wants and needs, then you do not even know what type of people to hire. So figure out what you are looking to solve and what type of future you would like to create for your business.

Then you can start to look at people. People are the biggest assets for a company. Having one very talented person is ten times better than having several average people. You want to make sure that you have the most talented people because they will do more work, and better work, than average and not-so-average workers. It also means you do not have to hire as many people. It is better to have three to five people within a team because it reduces the communication problem. The best layout for businesses and teams is to have small groups of very talented workers. It will work out better for your business to have two people who perform sixty hours each week than four working forty hours a week. You will save money and have more work done.

Then, it is important to look at your structure. Many businesses are centralized. This means you have the main person, the CEO, which everything must go through. When a business first starts out, and there are only a couple of other people working for the CEO, a centralized structure works fairly well. But the more people who start working, the crazier it becomes. It is best, then, to move to a decentralized organization structure.

Decentralized means you break the company up into its different functions. This could mean things like a sales team, customer support, product, and so on. Each of these groups will get their own team leader. This means that the people on the sales team just have to go to the team leader instead of to the CEO. If the team leader needs more information, they can contact the CEO.

The next thing to look at is the environment of the workers. Open-plan offices are typically a very bad idea. While they may look nice and friendly, they are not the most conducive for work. An open office plan causes distractions. If one person is focused on working and something happens elsewhere, it could easily distract them. If one person starts talking, everybody will hear it. There are no barriers to an open office.

That said, completely closed off offices are not always that great either because they are not conducive to communication? Therefore, you need to find a middle ground between the two. Having the office building broken down into sections separated by walls is a good starting place. Within those sections, you should have people who need to work together. Using glass walls is a good idea as well. It keeps things closed, but it also keeps it more open. Having open communal areas, like a cafeteria, is a good idea as well. Ultimately, you must figure out what setup works best for you. Distraction is the worst thing for a business. That is why it is important to partition the office off.

The last thing you must look at is content. The best thing to improve communication within the content is transparency. When you are completely transparent with what needs to be done, then it removes the need for communication. This means they will not have to ask for something. They can just get what they need. Companies do not have to hide everything from their employees. Things that are not sensitive should be transparent to people. It eliminates many problems. Instead of having an open office plan, have an open information plan.

Also, it is never a good idea to interrupt a person. Interrupting is not okay, ever. Let people work when they are working. Nobody should distract a person from working, especially if it is something important. Interruptions happen a lot in businesses. People in one team should not talk to another team. If a team member needs something from another team, they should speak with their team leader.

Individual teams do not have to check in with other teams to work on things. As long as there is one single source of truth for the people in the business, then everybody should be able to work on what needs to be worked on. It is okay if not everybody in the business is always on the same page. People in sales do not have to know exactly what people in HR are doing. This can all be achieved by having your own language. Special codes, acronyms, and the like can be helpful in sharing information and make sure that everybody is working toward the same goal for the business.

All this comes together to help prevent the breakdown of communication and to increase productivity. Communication should be addressed through the structure of the business so that people do not constantly have to ask other people what needs to be done because communication is the death of the business. This may not seem easy, and it is not, but with a few changes that I have mentioned, you will start to see improvement in your business's productivity.

Conclusion

Thank you for making it through to the end of *Time Management*. I hope it was informative and provided you with all the tools you need to achieve your goals, whatever they may be.

Procrastination is a problem, and it kills productivity, but it does not mean you are lazy. Everybody strives for productivity. People just want to get things done that they need to, but sometimes it does not happen that easily. By using the information, you have learned in this book, you can increase your productivity and decrease your procrastination. You will also find that you will have more time to do the things you like to do. Do not sacrifice your life or time trying to talk yourself into doing something. Use this book and just get it done.

Finally, if you found this book useful in any way, a review on Amazon is always appreciated!

www.ingramcontent.com/pod-product-compliance
Lightning Source LLC
Chambersburg PA
CBHW070049230426
43661CB00005B/829